Freedom Catalyst

Copyright © 2024 by Perception Concepts

All rights reserved. No part of this book may be reproduced or used in any manner without written permission of the copyright owner, except for the use of quotations in a book review.

To request permissions contact the publisher at info@perceptionconcepts.net

Second paperback edition October 2024
ISBN-979-8-9861517-7-9

Library of Congress Control Number: 2022910079

Contents

CHAPTER 1: The System and the Structure   1

CHAPTER 2: Three Phases of Mind   19

CHAPTER 3: Control Your Emotions   35

CHAPTER 4: Play the Game   49

CHAPTER 5: Hedge Your Bets   61

CHAPTER 6: Knowledge and Intention   71

CHAPTER 7: Acceptance of Fate   85

CHAPTER 8: Skin in the Game   97

CHAPTER 9: Awareness   113

CHAPTER 10: The Point of No Return   131

CHAPTER 11: Conclusion   141

Although the publisher and the author have made every effort to ensure that the information in this book was correct at press time and while this publication is designed to provide accurate information in regard to the subject matter covered, the publisher and the author assume no responsibility for errors, inaccuracies, omissions, or any other inconsistencies herein and hereby disclaim any liability to any party for any loss, damage, or disruption caused by errors or omissions, whether such errors or omissions result from negligence, accident, or any other cause.

This publication is meant as a source of valuable information for the reader, however it is not meant as a substitute for direct expert assistance. If such a level of assistance is required, the services of a competent professional should be sought.

The publisher and the author do not make any guarantee or other promise as to any results that may be obtained from using the content of this book. You should never make any investment decision without first consulting with your own financial advisor and conducting your own research and due diligence. To the maximum extent permitted by law, the publisher and the author disclaim any and all liability in the event any information, commentary, analysis, opinions, advice and/or recommendations contained in this book prove to be inaccurate, incomplete or unreliable, or result in any investment or other losses.

FREEDOM CATALYST PREFACE

Thank you for allowing me to offer this knowledge and these concepts to you. I genuinely hope that they are received well in directing you to a life of freedom and understanding. A heightened level of awareness can be achieved by implementing and following through with its lessons, and that awareness is liberation. Having the concepts described herein available to you when you have questions that need answers will also give you the confidence you need to move forward with intention.

Have you already begun to question everything? Are you seeking direction and understanding? To reach your desired outcome we will have to take a journey together, a journey for self-awareness while confronting your perception of reality, to awaken and inspire you to find the endless possibilities of what life can be, through which you will create your path to freedom.

Some knowledge should be achieved before a direction is created. This book is laid out to give some historical and financial information to start the journey, because this is a book about awareness, and these subjects need to be understood to make you think about why you should want to take the journey in the first place. I hope that you will take the descriptions and the points of view to realize that we are all in the same boat, before I describe the ways to build your own.

*Dedicated to all the "lost souls"
who were never lost in the first place*

"I went to the woods because I wished to live deliberately, to front only the essential facts of life, and see if I could not learn what it had to teach, and not, when I came to die, discover that I had not lived. I did not wish to live what was not life, living is so dear; nor did I wish to practice resignation, unless it was quite necessary. I wanted to live deep and suck out all the marrow of life, to live so sturdily and Spartan-like as to put to rout all that was not life, to cut a broad swath and shave close, to drive life into a corner, and reduce it to its lowest terms..."

- Henry David Thoreau

CHAPTER 1

The opening quote by Henry David Thoreau was published in 1854. It underpins his retreat to the solitude of Walden Pond. 170 years ago, Thoreau recognized that many had traded the richness of life for the trappings of material success, a mindset that remains prevalent today. He observed how people, in their desperate quest to secure their futures through mortgages and property ownership, had unwittingly shackled themselves to the very systems that drained their vitality. These self-imposed obligations—the weight of debt, the endless hours of labor—kept them from experiencing the true essence of life, leading instead to what he called "*lives of quiet desperation.*"

Breaking free from society's burdens can ignite a profound shift—a quiet yet powerful awakening that brings a deep sense of peace and clarity. This moment of liberation offers a glimpse of what it means to live life on your own terms, unburdened by external constraints. It's a deeper journey toward understanding and true freedom, where you are free to push the limits of life or simply be, without constraint. But this feeling of true freedom doesn't come easily; it requires time, understanding, and an openness which allows the weight of the world to drop from your shoulders.

Suddenly, you feel like the center of everything, living in the moment, and the day becomes yours. You see the world through a whole new lens, a world in which all the pieces move and work together. A world where you are part of an amazing, perfectly flowing energy working through every means at its disposal. Anything can happen at any time, and you no longer fear what will come. The weather is what it is, where you are is where you are, what will happen will happen, and you embrace it all. The experiences, the challenges you face, the people you meet, and the stories you share help you grow as a person. True freedom exists, and it's a feeling everyone deserves to experience.

I personally experienced such an awakening on one particular day in October, as I awoke in Allegheny National Forest, Pennsylvania, and took a dip in the Clarion River. There was no one around. I drove up to a little town called Ridgway, where I had breakfast surrounded by cheerful faces and had a nice conversation with an older man about life, the weather, his family, choices made in life, and anything else random strangers in a small town would talk about.

From there, I drove up to New York State, a place I'd never been to before, then on to Niagara Falls outside of Buffalo. Driving to the falls was so much easier than I thought it would be, considering it was New York State and a city I didn't know. I went to Niagara Falls State

Park, saw the falls, and then decided to take the "Maid of the Mist" boat tour. It was amazing!

I then searched for a place to stay for the night and found a campground not even twenty minutes away. The drive was spectacular, and there were very few people on the road, so I took my time following the river in the late afternoon. When I got to the campground, I found that there weren't too many others around, and I was surprised at how cheap it was compared to some others that I had stayed at, and this park was pristine.

To catch a sunset over Lake Ontario had me running through the woods like a kid in a candy store. I hadn't run through the woods like that, I thought, since I *was* a kid. I headed back up to camp and set up my tent for the night, still in shock at how amazing this place was and what a day I'd had. I thought, "Maybe I can find a place to get some food," and wouldn't you know, there was a bar and restaurant about three minutes away where I had a great time playing pool, conversing with the locals, and having dinner.

Every day has in store for you whatever it has in store for you, and that was such a great day that I could've died, and I would've been able to accept it! It makes me feel bad for those who perceive their lives as being so horrible that they would rather die than live, but there is a flip side to that coin, which is that one could have such an existence that they would be willing to die because they *had* lived.

The System and the Structure

It's a mess! At times, it seems like society doesn't want you to be free. How many people refer to life as "running on a hamster wheel"? Is that life? Is that what life should be? I don't think so. Could it be possible to find a balance between the rat race and the gypsy road? For as long as I can remember, my aspirations have been simple: to build my own home, cultivate a garden, and raise a family in peace. But I was soon confronted with the harsh reality that even such modest dreams are obstructed by government mandates. Despite the labor and sacrifice required to secure or construct a home, the relentless demands for permits, taxes, and fees have ensured that I would never truly be free from the system's grasp. Thus began my introduction to the system, my enslavement to it, and the unnecessary evils I've had to face as a part of it—evils that have eroded the possibility of living a truly simple and independent life.

While not all systems are inherently good or bad, we need to create our own systems and structure them accordingly. For personal development, this means creating our own individual systems that align with our unique goals, principles, and aspirations. Systems have been used as a method of control; now, let's use them as a method of liberation. Systems are essential for productivity and efficiency, and structure is important for confidence and focus. What truly determines success is the systems—the daily routines, habits, and processes—we put in place to reach our goals. *"We don't rise to the level of our expectations; we fall to the level of our training." - Archilochus*

Many of us who refer to our work life as "running on a hamster wheel" continue to do so without envisioning what we would prefer to do instead. Why is that? There seems to simply be a lack of options. We were set on a path that led to this place and taught to be this way. If you try to change the path, there are roadblocks everywhere that encourage you to stop trying and just continue with the status quo.

We look forward to a life of luxury in retirement, willing to sacrifice our entire lives for it. That dream is alive for all of us, even when we have nothing saved, nothing invested, and no way to generate the income necessary for that vision. Yet we still imagine our "golden years" when we will be free to live the life of our choosing. This idea has been implanted in our minds—another distraction.

Will you be cliff-jumping in another country, feeling the essence of life when you're 75? Hard to imagine. And what will you think of on your deathbed? A life of adventure and perseverance? Or a life of mediocrity, following the other sheep. Will you be at peace with yourself? Satisfied that you have done what you intended to do and are prepared for the next journey? You can't take any of it with you when you go, so if life will flash before your eyes when the end comes, begin now to make sure it's something worth watching.

As I write this book, I imagine going back in time and speaking with myself years ago and the many others I have met along the way—confused, lost, stuck, and burdened by a lack of knowledge, understanding, and options. Many of us are trapped in a vicious cycle, wondering what to do. You have to break that cycle, seek out the answers, and find true understanding.

But this is extremely difficult when you're stuck in that cycle, becoming more and more trapped and hopeless each day. The system created around us can make people feel so stuck, alienated, or lost that they contemplate ending their lives because it feels so miserable. It's completely unnecessary. That's why I say that death after a free and liberating experience in life is the flip side of that coin of despair and tragedy that we hear so much about.

This is our fault for being lost as a society in the first place—because of the people we idolize or hand power to, and the manner in which they behave. The information we know about corruption and lobbying for special interest groups, which sway policy against the majority interest of the people, or the creation and degradation of currencies, which enslave people for generations. Is this really the culmination of our existence in this place? Starvation, war, death, and a lack of education. With so much information available in the world, why are we, as a species, becoming dumber?

Why do we empower people to continue to portray ignorance and vanity as a hierarchy in society? There are many great role models who humbly follow their passions for admirable causes and societal education. Why don't we revere *them*? Are fortune, fame, and position really of higher value than education, awareness, and kindness for a self-aware form of life on a planet which has allowed it to exist for a brief moment in time?

I want to share the concepts I've learned from my own journey of seeking so that maybe someone out there can take the information without the journey and begin to change their outlook and direction now. If it helps anyone else, it will be worth it.

Free·dom:

The power or right to act, speak, or think as one wants without hindrance or restraint.

What does freedom mean to you? By definition, it is power. Think about that word for a moment, "Power." The natural historical course has been for some to gain power through many different ventures and schemes, and once acquired, it then creates an opportunity to reduce competition for it. These paths lead to struggle, inequality, anger, resentment, destruction, revolution, a reset, and the whole thing begins again to perpetuate itself throughout time.

Society, in many ways, does not want you to be free. Even if you step out of the box to begin to understand and express yourself, you are chastised for not staying in the same place, with the same job, and questioned like a criminal. We've lost the sense of commonality, community, faith, and trust. Too many people have taken advantage of the system, and those bad apples have spoiled the whole bunch. To get anywhere in that system now, you're expected to march through a predetermined sequence of tasks like a robot, but I won't accept it. This is my life, your life, our lives! And we're going to find a way through the mess that has been made.

Nobody wants to be trapped in the dark alone, so even the other sheep will try to keep you in your place. Many people don't seem happy. It's not all the time, and there are masks to wear, but inside, they just don't seem happy. What we need to strive for is to accept *some* bad moments in life with an understanding that pulls us through them, as opposed to having *some* good moments in life and the rest being just a constant, repetitive, and boring cruise toward the end.

Imagine waking up with approximately ten years left to live on this earth, looking back at some seventy years with only a few memories that invigorate your soul. We have been conditioned to believe in a concept of what freedom is, yet this idea is nothing more than a shiny prison constructed out of an illusion, meant to keep the masses controlled and reduce competition for power.

We Live Within Our Means

Whether you have five dollars in change in your pocket or fifty thousand in your bank account, you find a need and a way to manage it either way. We live within our means. The more we make, the more space we have, competition, events, friends, and then "keeping up with the Joneses" leads to an increased need to satisfy our lifestyles. What we need versus what we want or are accustomed to having are entirely different things.

Creating the means to live while understanding what is truly necessary requires thoughtful introspection. Every decision you make brings you closer or further from your ultimate goals. Are you simply a consumer, or can you educate yourself on the consequences of your choices and make decisions that propel you toward achieving freedom and changing your circumstances? If you are not just a consumer, then strive to become a creator—a creator of your own destiny. Many individuals avoid this path out of fear of not fitting in with their social circles or societal norms, preventing them from breaking free and discovering their true selves.

We live our lives day by day because we "can't see the forest for the trees." Like a mouse in a maze, we operate on instinct, focusing on basic needs like eating, sleeping, and reproducing. Imagine you're the mouse. What is your nature? Are you simply navigating the maze in search of the next reward, or are you driven by a purpose you have defined for yourself?

When surrounded by walls that limit your perspective, you may find yourself trapped in a cycle, influenced by external forces. If you could see it from a different point of view, you would realize that you're wasting time walking in the wrong direction. What if someone picked you up by your tail, and as you ascend from the box, you see the whole picture in plain view? Would you begin to understand?

Cat·a·lyst:

an agent that provokes or speeds significant change or action.

There comes a time in everyone's life when the familiar suddenly feels constraining, as if the walls that once protected us have become the very barriers that keep us from growing. It's in these moments of discomfort that true transformation begins. A catalyst jars your reality and forces you out of the box. There are many who have different concepts, striving to be different from what is considered "normal." They are considered "lost," always searching, trying to explain, and trying to motivate others. For those, including myself, no one gently picked us up from the box—the box itself was flipped off the table! And at that moment, being forced out of the box, we've all had to try to understand just what it was that we were looking at.

A constant in the awareness that comes from these catalysts has a lot to do with extreme loss and/or fear. Historical, religious, and philosophical references to pain, loss, destruction, and fear that had to be overcome as a staple in the structures of faith, philosophy, or fellowship. The Roman philosopher Seneca stated, *"Set aside a certain number of days during which you shall be content with the scantiest and cheapest fare"* describing a situation in which you face your fears and disconnect yourself from your possessions to realize that they do not define you. This practice promotes humility and stability, as the Chinese proverb goes: *"It is better to be a warrior in a garden, than a gardener in war."*

These examples highlight a similarity between cultures that coincide with simple ideas. These ideas can be understood by anyone who is willing to follow a path of understanding and make the attempt to step outside of the box. I will make my best effort to gently grab you by the tail and elevate you from the box so that, with a different point of view and a little effort, you can shift your perception from chasing that scent while caged in walls, to ascension and understanding.

It's in our most vulnerable moments that we often encounter the catalysts that challenge our perceptions and force us to confront our deepest fears, and it's through these challenges that we discover the strength to redefine our understanding of the world and our place within it.

The process that led me to this understanding, in retrospect, was an accident. These things happened in such a way that the impact prompted me to reflect on the concepts and feelings that I derived from them, a cause and effect, leading to the realization that:
1. I had to lose, and accept the loss of everything I thought defined me.
2. I had to be free to do anything and go anywhere.
3. I had to journey with no direction, seeking a knowledge of self.
4. I had to understand that I may not make it back, and accept that fate.

On that journey, I visited family members, friends, and close acquaintances, and tried to gain direction from that, but I also let events and acquaintances I met along the way dictate my direction (I *let go* of the wheel). Many questions arose that I will go into detail on because they became an important and integral part of the process of what I discovered.

It's about embracing acceptance to the fullest extent by flowing with life and confronting mortality, letting go of all attachments, and facing the fear of the unknown while acknowledging what you can and cannot control. Recognizing that you don't need, you don't want, and not only that, but the unnecessary and sometimes repugnant aspects of the situation we're in can often be disheartening. Why are we this way? How will we, as a species, ever be able to change the narrative? Too many of us are stuck in a box, unable to escape because we are trapped by things that seem to be beyond our control, affected by the way we view reality and how we respond to it.

While many strive for change, true transformation may only come from a significant catalyst. In the meantime, I urge you to pursue personal freedom and happiness while striving to be a positive force for change. Just as you must secure your oxygen mask on an airplane before assisting others, focus on your own growth first.

I'm going to describe some information and some concepts to help you get an idea of how to move in the right direction. The place that I want you to ultimately reach is simple to achieve; however, it's only a simple idea in hindsight. It's extremely difficult, in the environment that we all live in, to get there.

Freedom • Catalyst

Why should we take the journey? I grew up believing that if you want something, you should get a job, earn money, and then buy it. But after my own catalyst, I realized how widespread this pattern is: people working multiple jobs just to survive, often feeling miserable. Thousands upon thousands of people in cars, like zombies—filled with noise, anger, and devoid of consistent appreciation for the beauty that surrounds them—thinking this is normal... and I was one of them, even though, deep down, I always knew I needed to be free or pursue work that I truly enjoyed.

A problem I encountered is that even when you do what you love, there always seems to be someone there trying to turn it into just another "job" for you. How is a person supposed to better themselves when every moment of their time is taken up, and any capital they would need has been exhausted? Exactly! They're *not* supposed to. As long as the wheel is moving and you're running on it, you won't be free. As long as you're running and preoccupied, this stream runs down the hill with nothing to dam it up. That is, until you make a decision to do something about it, for yourself.

This is no easy task; it requires discipline, knowledge, patience, and time. Too many hurdles for most to overcome. It's easier to watch movies, eat junk food, and get intoxicated to forget what's happening. Think of the Roman Colosseum, filled with patrons of society releasing their frustration and anger on a distraction. The games were typically funded by the emperor with the *intent* of distraction. When the reality of the situation is out of your sight, it's also out of your mind. *"Give them bread and circuses and they will never revolt." - Juvenal (2nd century Roman poet)*

For What It's Worth

Ancient Rome also debased their pure silver coins with bronze and inflated them away, causing turmoil, death, and steering one of the greatest economic powers of all time toward collapse. Mike Maloney references this in his video series "*Hidden Secrets of Money*," which is a valuable educational reference.

I want you to realize that many countries in history that created more of their currency while still representing the value of what it once was, have seen similar fates. Following the ideas of previous generations, working in trade for a suitable existence, home, family, and retirement is not the same as it once was because of this degradation. It's important moving forward to educate yourself on these realities until you completely understand them. This way, you can make better decisions toward your challenging goals. To get started, take the time to watch "*Principles for Dealing with the Changing World Order*" by Ray Dalio.

Imagine a Roman coin that could initially buy a good or service but was later debased to only 5% of its original silver content. It would then take 20 of these debased coins to buy the same good or service. If workers' wages were still based on the premise that the coins were 100% silver, their income would effectively stagnate. This scenario has been playing out in the United States and globally for over fifty years, leading to stagnant wages, diminishing returns, and escalating living costs. It's the working class who are disproportionately affected, and as described in the beginning: struggle, inequality, anger, resentment, and revolution become the outcome, perpetuating the cycle again and again.

In a healthy economy, citizens produce and sell goods and services, using their incomes to purchase other products and services, thus creating opportunities and a robust economy. However, if the velocity of money slows and most people can't afford goods and services, economic activity grinds to a halt. The wealthy alone cannot sustain the economy. For example, a store that used to sell 100% of its products to the working class might now only sell 10%, unable to cover wages or overhead costs, leading to higher unemployment, exacerbating the problem. To understand more about the middle class's role, watch "*Saving Capitalism*" with former U.S. Secretary of Labor Robert Reich.

Inflation from currency devaluation has far-reaching consequences. It silently erodes individuals' purchasing power and destabilizes economies. Governmental decisions for checks and balances, including currency creation, impact inflation. When currency value decreases compared to its commodity basis, inflation becomes an *additional* tax which is imposed without representation, and it's the ordinary citizens who bear the brunt of the impact. Even wage increases meant to compensate for inflation often push individuals into higher tax brackets, keeping their real income stagnant.

This also affects retirement planning. If you plan your retirement expecting $1,000 a month for expenses, but inflation doubles the cost, your retirement funds won't last as long. Additionally, as you age, earning extra income becomes more difficult. This is a critical juncture where education and awareness play pivotal roles. This is about empowering individuals to understand the forces shaping their economic realities and charting a course toward financial resilience. If we continue in the current direction, many people may not even be able to *afford* to live, and those with nothing to lose could create extreme situations that put many others in danger.

We'll be facing significant societal issues in the near future, such as population, water, global changes, food supply, sustainability, and disease. It appears that those in power invest immense resources in controlling these commodities and cures, while the majority remain engrossed in distractions and consumerism. Consider how reliant you are on your job, your home, the food you eat, and the water you drink. What if these necessities were used against you? Most of us don't trust the people in power, who have the means to control these necessities. That's not a functioning society; that's being convinced and controlled. Many are aware of the greed, corruption, and influence of certain institutions, recognizing that these entities do not serve our best interests or our communities.

You don't have to be a slave to society to be productive, happy, or a part of it. This is about questioning norms and redefining what true freedom means. It's about dismantling the proverbial box society has placed us in and forging our own path forward. Breaking free from the confines of complacency and consumerism requires courage and conviction. Do you believe you're smart enough to manage your own life? You might think you've got it all figured out—you live in a nice area, work all week, pay your bills, follow trends, and enjoy weekends with friends. But is that how you would describe freedom when asked, "What does freedom mean to you"? If not, then it's your "BOX." Let's discuss how to break free from the box you have been placed in.

CHAPTER 2

"Read this text thinking that it is written for you; do not think that you are just reading or learning written things. Instead of imitating what I write, make this text yours, like a principle that you have brought forth from your own thought. It is necessary to ponder well by putting yourself into the situation."

- Miyamoto Musashi

It's not enough to realize that some people seem to understand more about financial literacy, business, or investments; you also need to know why. My parents are extremely hard-working and fun-loving individuals, and because of that, so am I. It's the example that I observed when my mind was taking in information as a child, so I always feel the need to do a "job." Using this example, it became apparent that unless I could convince my mind that my "job" was to become financially literate, it wouldn't be a priority. Whatever job I have will be the priority because that's what I was taught. I can learn anything if it's related to the job that I'll be doing in terms of traditional labor, but when I tried teaching myself about subjects such as finance or government at first, the same drive and vigor for learning just weren't there.

Realizing the difference between one dinner table and another, and understanding that while some witnessed talk about mortgages, rates, yields, real estate, or stock market returns, many of us just weren't at that table. Once a person can comprehend what is happening in their own mind, why the system we're in is structured the way it is, and how to create a new way of thinking to manifest their own destiny, they can begin to manifest change within their personal reality.

Three Phases of the Mind

There are three phases of the mind: the conscious, the subconscious, and the unconscious. Here is a simple description of how they work:

The conscious mind serves as the basic intake and delivery system. The eyes, nose, ears, and other senses take in information from the environment and send it to the subconscious mind for interpretation. This process occurs constantly, with the conscious mind handling immediate awareness and decision-making.

The subconscious mind acts as the 'key master,' acquiring knowledge and using that data to perform tasks like driving, brushing your teeth, and other routine activities. The subconscious can operate concurrently with the conscious mind, for example, allowing you to think about different things while driving. Its primary function is to store information from the past to make the body aware of familiar things, like "yes, this is cheese," and makes up approximately 50-60% of the mind.

The unconscious mind is where we face significant challenges. It comprises about 30-40% of the mind, but it's arguably the most influential. It holds the information stored from our early years, shaping our behaviors and motivations. This part of the mind influences the conscious mind, often without our awareness, in decisions such as the "fight or flight" response.

Consider a mouse, driven by instinct to eat, sleep, and reproduce. The unconscious part of the brain effortlessly guides these hereditary traits for survival in nature. However, as humans, we don't always align with the natural order. The unconscious mind relies on early teachings, passed down through generations, which may not always be reliable.

Understanding these mind phases sheds light on how society functions. By instilling a structure that teaches conformity, society can guide individuals to follow a set path, conforming to norms and expectations. This perpetuates a cycle where individuals repeat learned behaviors, often without questioning their origins.

In 1984, Yuri Alexandrovich Bezmenov gave an interview to G. Edward Griffin in which he described a process he called "a great brainwashing"—a slow process known as either ideological subversion, active measures, or psychological warfare. Speaking as a defected former KGB agent, Bezmenov outlined four basic stages to this process. The first stage, called "demoralization," Bezmenov stated, "*A person who has been demoralized is unable to assess true information. The facts mean nothing to him.*"

This shift in consciousness has led to societal systems that prioritize profit over virtue, widening the gap between social classes. Long ago, school systems were structured to create soldiers and workers, a corporate-style top-down intentional effort to destroy the will of the students, and that system has not changed in over 100 years. But if what I'm saying is correct, then why *would* it change? It's easier to keep a mass of people moving in the same direction. All that is necessary is to create a structure that teaches a child to get up, go to work, save money, not complain, follow the rules, and be happy with mediocrity. *Then* you'll retire someday, and *then* you'll be able to enjoy your life. You've just been dropped into the maze and told there is cheese (if you can find it).

Humans, unlike other creatures, must also navigate conflicting instincts and self-awareness. We ponder our appearance, perception, future plans, and societal expectations, creating a complex internal struggle. Understanding our instincts allows us to harness them for personal growth, but it also creates a constant tension between our primal urges and the demands of modern society. To address this internal conflict, we must first acknowledge the root of the issue and then work to change our ingrained thought processes. The challenge lies in overcoming the deeply rooted beliefs stored in the unconscious mind, which were established long ago and are resistant to change due to their perceived importance for survival.

Having this kind of information gives you tools to take control of your own life. However, it is also information that those who would control *your* life understand as well. Recognize that we are animals that need to eat, sleep, and breed because it is in our DNA. If we had been taught simple techniques to use with a mentality of perfecting those techniques for survival, we would be part of the sustainable chain that is the wheel of life. At some point, however, we started to become aware, consciously aware, and everything changed from there. Now we battle between what is in our nature and what is in the structured systems we have created.

Restructuring of the Mind

How can we restructure something that does not want to be restructured? We create habitual systems that we repeat over and over until the mind restructures itself for the betterment of the being. Let's use exercise as an example. A conscious decision must be made, followed by establishing a daily routine. Once you begin to see the physical benefits, you will be motivated to continue living that way because it is beneficial for you.

Even so, you'll experience situations where this is happening and you revert back to lounging, entertainment, and junk food. Why does this happen? Laziness? No, it's just not in your original programming, but watching TV and eating junk food probably is. Are you beginning to understand? It's a means of manifesting evolution. You have to determine what it will be, tell it straight to the mind, *why* it needs to change from what it is, and then maintain consistency with it until it becomes what you want it to be.

Change doesn't happen overnight; you have to catch yourself if you're falling back into unhealthy ways, whether that is old patterns, habits, or whatever the case may be. It takes time to break those cycles, just as it took time to create them, because you can't help being who you are from what you've experienced.

If you want to change it, you'll need a clear picture of what you want it to be, constantly correcting yourself, and motivating yourself through faith in your ability to make it happen. Who knows what you want more than yourself? Remove distractions like TV, video games, and the internet. Find a place that encompasses something natural, greater than yourself, and go there by yourself. Open your mind to the experience. Think about the history of whatever it is and realize how long it took to become what it is—the forces that shaped it, the outside world's influence on it—and relate its lessons to your personal world. Recognize your fragility and weakness. Do this as often as necessary until you can return with the information you need to create a persona that embodies the ideas that come to you from that place of humility and understanding. The knowledge that comes is from your own perception and the questions you didn't even know you had.

I once sat under a tree imagining its age and how it came to be there. I thought to myself: "If we are approximately the same age, then it has been here since I was born, learning its environment and gaining strength, while I've been jumping from metaphorical branch to branch." Just a passing thought, made meaningful because a catalyst gave me the perspective to consider what could be learned from nature. A catalyst can be created by taking the first step; it's not something that has to happen *to* you. In the words of RUSH, *"If you choose not to decide, you still have made a choice."* So it will be up to you to write your own story.

Governments and society are fooling you. Your mind, because of its foundation of teaching, is fooling you. When you realize this, you must reach out for knowledge about the nature of things and then begin to retrain yourself from a position of understanding, not a position of conformity. What we must do is tear down the old foundation that hinders our progress, so that we can build a strong unconscious foundation to construct a subconscious house upon, in which a conscious mind would be happy to live.

Making Sense of Consciousness

It's ironic that the statement "to make sense of consciousness" is that without self-awareness there would be no need to "make sense" of it. The simple fact is that no one truly knows *why* we are aware at all; in other words, what consciousness *is*. We've touched on the reality that the brain is functioning in a particular way to dictate your actions and that there is a struggle to understand why we as humans are so different from the other organisms that live on this Earth. We can use this as an opportunity to realize our own potential.

We've all heard of manifest destiny, and many ways to create your own reality, but what are some examples and how can we make that effort to affect our own lives? We excel through inspiration and desperation. When there is a need for something like food or water (a necessity) we become highly motivated to find a way to accomplish the goal, to acquire the need through *desperation*. This is when the mind will be forced outside of the box to become creative and solve the problem. When *inspiration* grabs hold of us, we become so determined to achieve the goals envisioned in our minds that we create desire. A strong enough desire to accomplish something can lead to extraordinary achievements, even those once thought impossible. This drive has enabled humanity to land on the moon, construct towering skyscrapers, cure diseases, and create global connectivity systems. Be sure to note that these past accomplishments required failure first, to create understanding before they could be accomplished.

Imagine becoming so excited to create something that it makes you feel driven to do anything to achieve it. An experience that helped me understand this concept was building a structure. I could clearly see the vision in my mind, and in doing so, I couldn't move fast enough or make enough money to achieve it as quickly as I could dream it. Because I was so dedicated to its creation and motivated by each stage of its progression, one day, there it stood, complete! I had created it, manifested it from my own mind, resources, education, and energy. But it's worth noting that these things take time. Patience is required to manage the anxiety that comes from wanting to see it accomplished, and the desire has to be so strong that you don't lose sight of the vision.

That project took me nearly four years to complete, with many hurdles and injuries (whether to myself or my pride) to overcome along the way. It taught me that patience, passion, and unwavering desire are essential for achieving a goal. Without passion, a vision, and the desire to create enough will to persevere, would it have come to fruition?

Completing a project over four years may seem like a lengthy process, but it teaches a valuable lesson: even with limited time, funds, and knowledge—having patience and desire allows you to keep pushing forward, enabling you to run on that "hamster wheel," playing the game while gradually grabbing small pieces of what you want, piece by piece, until the day comes when you've achieved your goal, whatever it may be. This is simply conscious effort, magnified. Understanding this concept will be a crucial step in your progression toward individual freedom.

Foundation of Self

Plants in the desert face harsh climates and must evolve to protect themselves. They grow slowly to ensure they do not exceed what the climate can sustain and develop sharp points or thorns for protection. Although these plants also produce flowers and play a role in the ecosystem, they must build defenses to survive in their environment. As you seek these answers, observe your surroundings, as they hold valuable insights. In this case, the key is to grow slowly with purpose, protect yourself, and contribute something beneficial to the world. To establish a foundation for yourself and your new "house," we will use the concepts outlined in this book as guiding instructions for decision-making.

An antenna for television or radio trying to pick up a signal is often filled with static or white noise, with many different communications passing by until that perfect frequency is acquired, allowing you to see the picture or understand the music. Each person has their own frequency, but internal noise—distractions, doubts, and fear—makes it hard to tune in. This is what I want you to imagine: a TV picture full of static, slowly coming into focus. To dial in on that frequency, you must educate yourself on the main principles. There are two essential questions you must answer: "Who are you?" and "What do you want?" It sounds easier than it is, believe me, but no journey can begin without a step.

You must simply ask these questions of yourself, over and over again, without the white noise. The white noise consists of thoughts like "What will people think?," "How will I be able to afford that?," "Where would I find the time?" etc. These questions are a completely different ballgame, like worrying about dangerous animals in the forest before you've even begun to hike. Don't worry about the animals in the forest; the question is simply, "Where would you like to go hiking?"

When you begin to ask these questions, the mind will go to work on them. They seem like simple questions but are very complex at the same time. When ideas come to you, write them down, then ask the questions again. The "middle person" (subconscious) will be working on this continuously from the moment you ask. As you start to change your own narrative, the subconscious will reach out to the unconscious for advice, and that advice will be that it does not fit the narrative or the need for survival in reference to lessons of societal structure.

It is up to you to retrain the system by jarring it over and over, by asking the questions again and again, allowing these buried ideas to resurface and guide you toward a path that aligns with your true desires and aspirations. By reading over these descriptions, you will find similarities, ideas, and aspects of yourself from deep within the mind that had not occurred to you because they have been suppressed, changed to fit a narrative of survival in your environment. You were inspired by them at some point, but they were never given room to grow due to disregard, other people's opinions, or fear. They are trapped in the subconscious mind, planted there from the moment of their creation, and doomed to stay useless because they don't fit the unconscious teaching and have not been brought to the forefront of consciousness for creation. As the subconscious mind digs deeper through your life's influences, motivations, and thoughts, these concepts and ideas will surface as potential answers to the questions you are asking.

Personal Growth

Sometimes, a significant event forces us to pause and reflect on our true desires. It is important to realize that personal growth should be based on self-reflection and understanding, not just following the status quo. Some individuals may pursue a career for financial gain, only to realize later that it does not align with their true passions.

Much of who you are currently may not align with who you aspire to be or what you want to achieve. This is where you understand the challenges of pursuing your goals and striving to become the best version of yourself. Challenging, yes. But once you've started this process, going back would mean defying what you have determined to be the real you and the true desires you have for this life—rather than conforming to what is perceived as acceptable or portraying someone you're not—which only brings unhappiness.

Should a person conform to the norm because of societal expectations, or should they follow their heart and do what feels right for them? That decision is yours to make. In my opinion, a major aspect of true freedom includes being where you truly want to be. Scientific studies have demonstrated that cultural and social norms prevalent in a location significantly influence individuals' happiness. Therefore, finding a location that aligns with your preferences—whether it's mountains, coastline, or urban areas—can notably increase your overall happiness and well-being. Maybe you're happy where you are, or maybe you just don't know, but exploring these preferences for yourself serves as the starting point for finding answers and embarking on a journey of seeking, understanding, and ultimately personal growth.

I see the pursuit of personal freedom like this: Imagine you are in a small boat in the ocean, with a large continent ahead of you and a small island in the distance. The island represents the life of freedom, personal exploration, and creativity you are striving for. The boat symbolizes you in your current position, while the large continent represents the "training" you have received and the expectations placed upon you. From the spot you're at to the island is your path, the path that you set for yourself. The vision is as simple as setting the boat on the course for the island, and the continent is only there for navigational purposes. At times when the waves are high or the fog is thick, the only concern you need to worry about is that you are maintaining that course.

When your mind is in that fog, it is important to understand that the boat has already been pointed toward the island (your path and goal). If you maintain your compass, have faith that nothing lies between where you are and where you will be, and keep your heading even through the fog, you will arrive at your chosen destination.

Education and Delineation of Goals

One of the biggest problems we have is a lack of education on subjects related to this foundation that we need. Anything we come together to solve as a community can be solved. If we focus on the problem, become educated on the reality of the situation, and work as a community to solve it, we can achieve it. While, as a whole, we have shown that we may not or will not do so, we can take the lesson to improve ourselves individually.

Everything you desire can be achieved through setting goals, taking the necessary steps to achieve them, educating yourself about their reality, maintaining consistency in your determination to follow those steps, and continuously self-checking to ensure you are on track. When you have a dream, turn it into a goal. Each natural step leads you closer to that goal, with each step itself becoming a goal, and each of those goals containing steps. These steps and goals ultimately lead you to your highest goal, your dream coming true—your island of freedom.

I posed the question, "What is freedom to you?" because although the definition of the word has been described, the concept is different for everyone. You could have financial independence that gives you the freedom to go and do whatever you want. You could also achieve freedom of mind through intellectual wisdom, such as a deep understanding of yourself and emotional control, allowing you to move through life as a wave moves through the ocean. Ideally, we strive for a combination of both. If you are not as free in your finances and continue to work within the system, your intellectual wisdom will allow you to see it for what it is, rather than being controlled by it, as you steer your boat in the right direction. Conversely, if one has financial independence without that intellectual wisdom, I would hope that somewhere along the way they naturally develop it. However, it rarely happens, in my opinion, due to an inability to control the ego and the consumption that accompanies it.

CHAPTER 3

"Learn how to be happy with what you have while you pursue all that you want."

- Jim Rohn

Don't overextend yourself or stray from your path. Discipline and focus may be challenging, but they are essential on your journey. With time, patience, and personal growth, you will be better equipped to navigate the obstacles that may arise. In nature, you can't control the elements, but you can anticipate them. It's not raining, but it could rain. It's not snowing, but it could snow. It's light out but it *will* get dark.

Control Your Emotions

Be free from the *passion* of emotion, not emotion itself. Self-regulatory psychology involves the ability to perceive, use, understand, manage, and handle emotions. It helps regulate attitudes and feelings that directly affect the development of self-control as a means of overcoming *destructive* emotions.

For a person to be able to assess a situation for the betterment of their future and themselves, they need to understand that outside forces often come to veer us off our path. Imagine for a moment that you're sailing your boat. You've become educated on how to sail, determined where you want to go, and braved the exhilarating moment when you set out on that course. But then, in comes that fog or those waves. What do you do? Stay calm and maintain the course. In these moments, we are building faith in ourselves and our desired destination. We are gaining experience from the tough times that will make us wiser in the future by not making poor decisions based on factors beyond our control.

learn to embrace the chaos in unpredictable or disorderly situations to encourage acceptance and adaptation as a philosophy toward resilience and flexibility. By recognizing that we cannot change external events, we can redirect our energy toward managing our internal responses, choosing how we interpret and react to situations, rather than allowing our emotions to be dictated by the external world. This way, you not only maintain your composure but also strengthen your resilience, helping you navigate life's uncertainties with a sense of calm and empowerment, ultimately leading to greater emotional stability and well-being.

Personal Development

Reflect on past experiences and consider how they have shaped your current path. Identify potential obstacles and make a plan to overcome them. Focus on positive growth rather than falling into self-destructive patterns. While it is important to meet societal expectations, it is equally crucial to stay true to yourself, set goals, and work toward achieving them.

Everything in our lives is a reflection of the choices we make. Each decision, whether conscious or unconscious, sets into motion a series of events that shape our experiences, relationships, and outcomes. Our circumstances, successes, and challenges are not mere happenstance, but reflections of our innermost beliefs, values, and actions. In the face of adversity or stagnation, we reclaim the power to redefine our paths and manifest the changes we seek if the underlying motivations behind our decisions align with our aspirations, values, and long-term goals.

Each moment presents an opportunity for growth. Understanding yourself and coming to peace with what you truly want while taking the necessary steps to become educated, experiment, explore, and learn can help you create the existence you desire by following the path less traveled. Embrace the role of architect in your own life, continually striving to cultivate and develop a future that resonates with authenticity, growth, and meaningful impact. By doing so, you may create a lifestyle similar to someone who focuses on building their dream from the widely traveled path. Choose which path aligns with your personality. Will you blaze your own trail, or follow someone else's path? Difficulties will arise no matter which direction you choose, so choose your difficulty. Will your challenge be in blazing a path for others, which may be difficult—or in following by imitation, which may appear to be easier, but lacking in individuality?

Practice compassionate and polite acts to promote emotional stability. One small daily effort toward a good deed will absolutely change your attitude. By focusing on improving your own life and self, those around you will treat you differently. People are naturally drawn to individuals who exude passion and joy, inspiring them to excel as well. According to Dennis Prager, "*People act more decently when they are happy.*" Alternatively, constantly being exposed to and focusing on the catastrophes of the world, when there is nothing you can do about it, is destabilizing and not helpful to you. If you focus on the negative, you may attract negativity, but positive thoughts breed positive actions

Play the game: run on the hamster wheel to meet the societal needs required to survive in your environment. At the same time, cultivate a sense of self, determine your desires, create a game plan, and navigate through that system. As one gains momentum, you will slowly back away from the other.

Expectations of Others

Don't stress too much about how others will react to your accomplishments. As you walk down this road of self-discovery and understanding, you will become excited, as if finding something magical that has been right in front of you the whole time and you just couldn't see it. However, if you're proud of something you've accomplished, expecting praise from others may lead to disappointment.

At times, people subconsciously do not want others to succeed, so as not to overshadow their own success. This is not as intentional as one might think; it's just ingrained in everyone's instinctive traits, similar to being the most colorful bird displaying the best mating dance ritual. The *analogous theory* in human behavior suggests that members of a group will try to diminish the self-confidence of any member who achieves success beyond the others. This behavior stems from envy, resentment, spite, conspiracy, or competitive feelings, all aimed at halting their progress. Instead of offering genuine support, others might subtly downplay your achievements by focusing on potential risks or failures.

If others don't share your level of enthusiasm and passion, and it makes you feel like you didn't do as good of a job as you thought, or that what you found won't be as magnificent as you think, don't be discouraged. It may be a subconscious ploy to lessen the beautiful dance that you're exhibiting. Stay true to your passion and hold onto that excitement. Eventually, your uniqueness will shine through, just like the most colorful bird with the best dance.

When you create a product or perform a service that you are passionate about, let the marketplace be your guide. Listen to feedback with an open mind, regardless of whether it's positive or negative, especially when it comes from those who have no vested interest in protecting your feelings. Use criticism as a tool for growth—an opportunity to educate yourself further and refine your skills. Don't internalize criticism as a judgment of your self-worth. Feedback can highlight areas for improvement that you might have overlooked. View it as constructive input that guides you toward excellence.

Pursue your goals for yourself, not to seek approval or validation from others. Accept criticism with grace, using it to become a better version of yourself without letting it diminish your confidence or self-esteem. Understand that each step forward, no matter how small, contributes to your ultimate success. Achieving meaningful goals takes time, perseverance, and a willingness to adapt. By keeping a balanced perspective, you cultivate resilience and ensure that your passion continues to drive you toward your ultimate aspirations. Confidence is there to guide you on your journey, but ego (yours *and* theirs) will also be there to destroy you.

Begin Building Your Structure

Imagine for a moment the home as a metaphor for the structure of the mind—your identity, your desires, and your aspirations. At this moment, you may not yet have a clear concept to describe, but as you begin to understand more about the true nature of yourself (what you want this house to look like), you can start sketching the blueprints. Take the time to design the house that represents you—the image of *who* you will become and the shape you want your life to take.

As you do your due diligence, your ideas will develop, and your blueprint will become more refined. Intuitively, you'll know when it's the right moment to seek help to bring that vision to life. Those who can assist you in your ventures—mentors or resources (your architects and engineers)—will become available once you seek them out. At this stage, your sketch begins to evolve into a more finely detailed version of the creation and realization of exactly what you want.

Reflect for a moment on the term structure; "To give pattern or organization to." You have learned the basic theoretical concept of what is happening inside the mind, and I really hate to say that the mind cannot always be trusted. However, the ideas in this book emphasize the importance of being aware of what is happening within and around you. Be cautious until you achieve that awareness, so you can create a solid structure that gives you the confidence to make decisions appropriately for yourself and your future.

You now know that the current theory of mental "foundation" that has been established is not going to be sufficient for the structure that needs to be constructed to achieve freedom and happiness. Whether a home is tiny or enormous, they all require a foundation of over-engineered strength to support what will be built on top of them and what could potentially be added to them in the future. If a foundation is not built to these standards, what happens to the structure above? Stress cracks form, external elements start to infiltrate the structure, and the home begins to deteriorate.

Reflect on "Expectations of Others" while realizing the metaphor in this scenario, in terms of stress, and external elements. Before we can construct this foundation of strength, we have to tear down the original one, because we only have that one piece of real estate to work with. Here are some suggested guidelines to outline the blueprint for your foundation, as you will want to see inspiring results that lead to further steps.

Find a consistent time to wake up in the morning and, if possible, a consistent bedtime to establish a regular sleep pattern. Avoid sleeping in or hitting the snooze button. Give yourself more time than you need, so that you will have moments for yourself and no one else. When you're waking up in the morning and rushing out the door while eating breakfast on the run, someone else is in control of your day, not you. By consistently starting your day at the same time with your own goals in mind, you are making decisions that lead to positive change.

I understand that the busy nature of life can make this challenging, but when your sleep schedule is disrupted, you can get fatigued, experience decreased alertness, or face issues with memory and decision-making. However, by consistently waking up at a set time, you help regulate your *circadian rhythm*. Eventually, you'll find that you no longer need an alarm to wake up at that specific time, and you will also experience better overall health and mental clarity. This is when you will start to see progress and realize that you have the power to make changes within your mind simply by taking charge of your day through your actions.

Make your bed. It doesn't matter if it's a mattress on the floor, a California king with eighteen pillows, or a sleeping bag. If a person were to leave for an extended period of time, it would be encouraged to clean the sheets, make the bed, do the laundry, clean the floors, pay the bills, etc. This idea is known as "*A place for everything, and everything in its place.*" This way, when the person returns from wherever they have gone, they find no obligations burdening them when their energy has been exhausted in other directions. It is a simple task that starts the day with an accomplishment, building momentum and reducing the burden on the mind. When done consistently, it can be seen by the conscious mind as an organization of the structure of your life. And what does conscious perception do with that information? It sends it to the subconscious for interpretation and storage. Each time you complete this task, remember that you are making a statement to yourself about control and organization. When you return from taking care of your daily obligations, or giving time to someone else's projects, you will see the control that you have over your own environment and projects, and the stress associated with daily life will be lessened.

Build a "game plan" for the next day the night before. The last thing you think of before you sleep will be the area of focus in the subconscious while the body rests. By consistently completing these simple daily tasks, you are creating positive structure in your life. As you prepare yourself to end this day and look toward the next, describe simply what you must focus on the next day and remind yourself generally of your major goals.

For example, you might say, "Tomorrow I need to contact this person, complete this project, or get started on this project. What's going to happen is that I will get to the completion of the 'X' goal and that will render X results. That result will assist in the direction of completing the 'Y' goal and that will render Y results. Then I'll be able to complete 'Z,' my main goal, and be successful in achieving my ultimate dream." When you open your eyes two minutes before that alarm goes off and immediately get out of bed, in control of the day with a plan to achieve what you set out to accomplish, your goals become achievable because you've shown yourself that knowledge, ideas, consistency, and structure will manifest change.

Perceptions

A simple concept to remember is to perceive the situation for what it is. If the situation has occurred in the past, it cannot be changed. Dwelling on it only leads to a form of depression, slowing down your progress.

If it is something that could potentially happen in the future, make your best efforts to guide the situation in your favor. However, remember that the future has not yet occurred, so don't create anxiety; create purpose and drive instead. If a progression of events doesn't go in your favor, refer to the information above because dwelling or overthinking on a future situation will create unhealthy anxiety that causes one to lose focus. So you see, most depression and anxiety (which seem to be the most common ailments of society today) stem from things completely beyond our control. *"When you change the way you look at things, the things you look at change." - Dr. Wayne Dyer.*

Things that happen to us in life sometimes happen *for* us. It's all about the mind's perception and interpretation. Just as thinking too much about the future can create anxiety, change your perception about what you consider is happening *to* you, to imagining that the tough path that you're on or the situation that you're dealing with is going to lead you to the place that you're supposed to be or give you the knowledge to conquer a future problem.

This positive mindset will give you the drive to move forward rather than the negative energy that pulls you down and takes you further away from your goals. Live your life in the moment, understanding what you can change to progress toward the fruition of the next goal in the progression of goals that manifest your destiny. Also, understand what is an unchangeable deterrent that creates regression and indecision. These are key components to living your best life. It's the difference between the path you're on and the path that you want to be on.

Within Relationships

We began this chapter with "Control Your Emotions" and end with "Within Relationships," which will undoubtedly be one of the most challenging tests on your journey. Controlling your emotions does not mean being selfish or heartless, *especially* within relationships. The goal is not to suppress your emotions but to manage them in a way that fosters a healthy and loving relationship. By recognizing and managing your emotional responses, you lay the groundwork for stronger communication and a deeper connection with others.

Let's reflect on what we've covered so far as we delve into this expansive and difficult subject, to see how these lessons provide insight. You've learned that "*to change your current situation to acquire something you want, you must reach out for a small piece at a time until it can be acquired in its entirety.*" Rushing in can damage the path that you're on. Patience and time build strength and clarity. You can gain an education without having to learn the hard way from harmful consequences to either party.

"*Understand who you are and what you want.*" If you have made up your mind about the direction you're going, find a partner for that journey. If you deviate from your path for the sake of the relationship, you may have to take a longer route to get back on course.

"*Become educated about the things you're interested in.*" Many people from many walks of life have different needs and ideas about what an ideal relationship is to them. Educating yourself on how to properly communicate your intentions, and how to understand the other person's intentions, will give you the tools to begin your work. "*If you don't find an intelligent companion, a wise and well-meaning person, going the same way as yourself, then walk alone. Like a king abandoning a conquered kingdom or like a great elephant in the deep forest. It is better to be alone than to be with those who will hinder your progress.*" - Buddha

A relationship can be incredibly beneficial in achieving your goals as a team, but it can also be detrimental if you get thrown off course, backtrack, and lose focus on yourself and your path. Learning to control your emotions will give you clarity and help you stay calm while maintaining your course. To stay on course, you'll need to assess and adjust your goals accordingly; these adjustments should make your main goal easier to achieve without changing the structure completely.

Many forces can set us off our path, such as losing loved ones, growing apart, or having our trust broken. If we stay educated and maintain our course, it will be easier to navigate through these challenges. Do it for yourself, and you'll have no regrets—only memories and wisdom.

Don't take things personally, whether within the relationship or after it. If you're in a relationship, educate yourself on the underlying causes of issues to build a stronger, more understanding, and supportive relationship through effective communication and active listening. If the relationship has ended, demonstrate maturity and integrity by seeking closure for your emotional well-being. Allow yourself time to heal and move on. Learning from the experience can help you grow and avoid similar issues in the future. Your journey toward self-discovery and personal growth continues regardless of the storms you encounter. Remember, just keep steering the boat.

Chapter 4

"God, grant me the serenity to accept the things I cannot change, Courage to change the things I can, and the wisdom to know the difference."

- Reinhold Niebuhr

Sometimes, a solitaire card game can be surprisingly flawless, and that's just the way it is; you don't have to overthink it. Other times, there is no way to win; you shuffle, try again, and still no win. There are some individual days like this, when nothing falls into place. You're putting in the effort but not accomplishing anything, where doing nothing would accomplish just as much, or more, than trying your hardest. However, these specific days are few and far between. They are different from situations that you can fight through. Sometimes, a reset is all that is needed for something to continue working. On days that seem like there is no way to win and you find that you are just digging a hole, it's very possible that it is within your control to just stop digging and reset instead.

Don't Give Up

We hear it all the time, "don't give up." That's easy to say, but it also happens all the time; we give up. Why? Because without the concepts presented thus far, patiently and consistently adopted and practiced, there is not enough confidence to push past the pitfalls and hurdles that naturally occur. They occur to inform, educate, enlighten, and direct you—not to deter you. If you're not perceiving it in that way, then you'll take its meaning as a deterrent and give up on this goal for something else.

If the day doesn't happen to start in your favor, or you notice that you're slacking and drifting away, it's not too late to get started and reset the best you can. Feeling too much anxiety or being depressed usually causes these kinds of drifts. Realize if it is a situation within your control to affect, hit the reset button, and start again. If it seems like the entire universe is rebooting and you just can't get a foothold even with a reset, you may have to completely stop, or focus on something very simple in an effort to achieve one small victory. But let it be. It's just a day.

Everyone loses at times—bad bets, bad choices. When a situation arises where you're going to lose, push yourself to do the work necessary to minimize the loss. Minimize the loss and make sure you learn the lesson associated with it so it doesn't happen again, and then move on. If you're walking down a path and come across a fallen tree or overgrown weeds, what would you attempt to do? Observe the situation, create a way around it, and get back on the path. These obstacles will arise constantly, testing your resolve, but don't let them stop you from starting or derail you from finishing.

I think of extreme situations like this as a vortex, like a black hole, or like quicksand. It's the opposition and it's pulling you in; you have to fight! Fight tooth and nail to get free because it wants you to give up. Whatever "*it*" is, wants you to think it's too hard. It wants you to think that it's unachievable, so that you let go, and it can take you in. Another victim of circumstance. We do better because of desperation as well, remember?

Keep your sights optimistic, believing that you're going to claw your way out despite the odds, that you're going to get free. Whether it takes time, distance, or money—no matter what it is—keep your mindset focused on the goal of escaping that vortex. Stay calm and think about the situation. If it's a black hole, you need to overcome the force with strength and power. But if it's quicksand, struggling too hard would create the opposite effect; a person would become tired and get sucked in. It would be the slow, consistent movement in that case that gets you out of the hole. So you see, it's in the knowledge of the situation you find yourself in that will give you the win because you are calm and intelligent, or powerful and determined, whatever the nature of the situation demands.

Like a bird landing on a high wire, everything moves—the wire and the entire body of the bird as it absorbs the energy of all that is changing around it. However, the head remains still, its sight focused on what it is perceiving and where it is going.

Moving Pieces to Places

You know that you want to exist within the system with freedom and happiness. You know that it is going to take education and effort to achieve. You understand why there is resistance in the mind, and how to effect change. You know that you must decide, for yourself, who you are and what you want. Your mind is calm because you begin to control your emotions, and now you know the best way to build a strong foundation for that happiness.

In the game of solitaire, much like life, you're playing a game to win and managing the cards along the way. You have to be aware of everything that's happening, or you could miss a move. By slowing down, observing the pieces, and contemplating the moves, you will find more options and make better decisions. Having basic principles as constants in life means understanding that every game is going to start the same way, with the same amount of cards (time in a day), and coupling those principles with the ability to be patient and wise is another key to your success.

Learn to communicate well. Your ability to move the cards in life will depend on how well you can move the pieces to the right places. Opportunities can be won or lost depending on how you communicate your intentions or navigate the situation. As you're playing, you're looking ahead, starting to see what cards you need, making decisions on which cards to move, and everything is based on one ultimate goal, like the goals you've created to take you to your highest goal.

What is white noise and what is part of your own frequency? There are many lessons that can be learned in solitude. You need to stop listening to the white noise first, and then condition yourself to recognize your own frequency. That frequency can't be honed in on when you're being affected by so many outside distractions. Just seeing your phone on your desk makes you more likely to pick it up. It's much harder to focus when you're tired or hungry, and when we push ourselves too hard, our brains naturally seek distractions as a way to take breaks (so try to take intentional breaks instead).

Now that you have some structure, start to build a routine. During moments of downtime or distraction, you may begin to experiment with some of these beneficial motivators and stress relievers that can help quiet an overanxious mind. Exercise releases endorphins and can make you feel calm and happy. Listening to certain music can drown out racing thoughts. Going for a walk or getting some sun can increase serotonin, which helps regulate mood, sleep, anxiety, appetite, and pain.

Journaling can help relieve stress and anxiety; a lot of thoughts and feelings that we have seem larger when held inside, but when observed from a different perspective, we're sometimes able to deduce them to a simpler truth and find resolutions. And of course, meditation helps you focus your attention, calm you down, and reduce overthinking.

One Card Can Change the Game

Getting to the position you want to be in life ultimately comes down to the decisions you make along the way. It's like playing a game of solitaire, where the cards are laid out on the table and that's what you have to work with. Imagine seeing six stacks of cards on the table, each representing different ideas for creating something useful for the world and for yourself.

As you look over the stacks and consider your next move, you notice that three stacks show the three, four, and five of diamonds, which could open up more opportunities to win the game if only you had the two of diamonds. There are two lessons to take away from this scenario. First, if you can find the two of diamonds, it will create a domino effect and increase your opportunities. Your focus shifts to figuring out how to move pieces around to create those opportunities. This is something within your control—asking yourself, "What can I do to open the doors of opportunity and find that two?" The ultimate goal is to win the game, but it's important to remember that it takes achieving smaller goals along the way. In this case, finding the two of diamonds is your current goal.

However, if you can't access the two because a move can't be made to retrieve it, and you end up running out of moves and losing the game, then the potential opportunities become irrelevant. Relying on just one piece to solve the puzzle, or one card to win the game, leaves you vulnerable and at risk of losing, as it puts you in a position with less control.

How You Play the Hand

"It's not whether you win or lose, it's how you play the game." What does that mean? It's a statement about always doing your best. When you lose, you learn, and when you win, you win! On to the next step or goal.

It's our goal to win, but we will lose sometimes. Did you do the absolute best you could? Did you miss something? How could you have played your hand differently? Take the loss as a learning lesson, store it in the subconscious, and move on. Failure is about learning to slow down, constantly observing situations, weighing them against the desired end result, and making decisions based on desired outcomes. Constants married with variables of chance.

Remember this: failure is as common an ingredient to a successful person as butter is to a chef. It's not "if you fail" it's "what do you do *when* you fail?" Do you pick yourself up and try again, or do you cower from fear of the next failure? Sometimes a loss can be caused by those unconscious "fight or flight" type reactions that drive people and opportunity away. Reactions that often lead you to mess up your intentions or cause you to manifest failure.

If you think for just a moment, I'm sure that anyone could come up with a personal example for this situation. Those times when you thought, "What am I doing?" or "Why did I do that?" This is a prime time to observe the situation and question why. There may be underlying causes buried beneath the surface that are making those decisions for you, completely unaware of how they affect your conscious life, and made as an "auto-pilot" decision.

This is why it is so important to understand what you want. Write it down, focus on it, and make the mind aware of it. Because if you don't have that ultimate goal, how do you play your hand, and what will you do when you lose? If you can learn how not to take things personally, knowing you did your best. Learn the lesson that is trying to be portrayed, through knowledge of the idea that things happen *for* you. And then jump right back in to play another game, so that you won't let the *unchangeable* past control your state of emotion and slow your progress. Then you'll get better and better at playing the game.

Odds

What are the odds? They are about 80/20. 80% knowledge and 20% variables or "chance." When you say (or hear someone say) that someone else got lucky, if you dive a little deeper, you'll come to find that either time, knowledge, or resources played a big role in that "luck." A person could have that 80% of time and knowledge invested and still get that 20% "bad luck" (the variable that could not have been considered because there is no history or playbook for it).

Depending on too few pieces to make the whole puzzle come together, or missing some of the pieces in the first place can ruin your success. So, even when all the angles have been considered, make sure to check yourself against the unknown "20%." This will help you remain humble and hedge your bets against a constant and consistent 20% variable that could be in your favor (lucky) or not (unlucky).

When bad things happen to good people, they automatically think, "Why me? I have the worst luck!" At these times, it's important to immediately stop beating yourself up and blaming situations that happen to you as bad luck. Instead, redirect your thoughts to the realization of the situation, that most likely what happened was due to a lack of knowledge, due diligence, or perseverance. These are variables that are within your control. Immediately change your perception from "happened to me" and "bad luck," creating negative energy and depressed feelings, and train your mind to think "happened for me," so that you can begin to understand your own lack of knowledge and take steps to become aware of the variables within the eighty percent that you had missed in your due diligence of the situation.

This will form a positive, problem-solving action to initiate in the mind as opposed to negative energy that is a drain on the mind as it becomes confused and depressed, searching for ways to cure bad luck, which is not regarding a situation as it truly is. This creates a scenario where you become less confident and depressed by situations that have already passed and cannot be repaired except through growth by perseverance, understanding, and knowledge seeking. The sooner you flip this switch, the less time will be wasted on self-pity directed at variables that are within your control and just need more understanding and patience to redirect in your favor. The calmness of mind and respect for the thing that you are trying to affect. Knowing that it's only a small percentage of variables and that the rest can be related to knowledge.

Bend, but Don't Break

Create more opportunities to increase your chances of winning the game. Give yourself additional paths to reach the same goal. Just as we've been taught to follow the rules by learning to color inside the lines or paint by numbers, make the realization for yourself that a solid yellow line on the road means nothing when no cars are around. Structured rules differ depending on which part of the world you're in, and just because the rules of the game are stated, there are ways to bend them.

Bend the rules as much as you can to help yourself. If it doesn't hurt anyone but will help you, expand your perception of things that can be affected by you, even if it seems contrary to the conventional way of doing things. You don't want to create harm or be reckless, but as you become more and more of a free-minded individual, you will begin to notice the rules that almost everyone follows, which you will be able to bend to your will because of your perception of the whole picture. This is a positive outcome of questioning, pushing boundaries, and understanding their true nature, which is an educational experience that occurs during self-awareness and learning.

It's a simple concept that you've been taught is wrong. Children naturally test limits. When a parent says "no," the child may continue to push those limits. By testing boundaries, they learn what can be achieved before facing consequences. Embrace this childlike curiosity. Remember, life is fleeting. You're living on a giant rock hurtling through space with minimal time to live, so don't take things too seriously, and understand where the real limits lie. Adapt the game to your advantage and always have a backup plan for when things go awry.

Chapter 5

"Drop by drop is the water pot filled. Likewise, the wise man, gathering it little by little, fills himself with good."

- Buddha

You're playing the game. You understand that working for someone else provides tools to reach your next level, whether it is money, experience, etc. Do your job well, but do your life better. Ensure your time dedication is primarily on creating the life you envision for yourself and the goals you have created to take you there. The time you trade for income by providing your work to someone else is just that, a trade of one thing for another. You've learned to stay humble and weigh the variables, not in a pessimistic way, but in a way that promotes safety and security by being able to move pieces to places by multiple means and hedge against the twenty percent should it drift in the wrong direction.

Don't Paint Yourself Into a Corner

Hope for the best, but prepare for the worst. Many situations we find ourselves in are avoidable, but we often don't realize we're putting ourselves in those positions until it's too late. Remember, we can't change the weather, but we can anticipate what might happen. Don't overlook possible scenarios or put faith in something you shouldn't, as it can lead to setbacks in time, money, or create anxiety and pain.

If you don't execute a plan with an end goal and an exit strategy, you may end up having to go over it again, go backward, take more time than necessary, etc. Bad situations happen to people all the time, and hard-learned lessons come from them. Like juggling two things in your hands, you can walk and talk and perform the tasks with ease, but when you decide to juggle more and more, then you are putting yourself into a position to drop something. Avoid the tendency to "paint yourself into a corner" to save time and trouble in the future.

Life's lessons can be difficult, and some lessons ultimately have to be learned through experiences. When these situations make it difficult to smoothly transition and take control of your next steps, you may have to rely on others to get back to stable footing, which can leave you vulnerable. Understand the direction you wish to travel so that you can make decisions based on how they move the needle in reference to that direction. Being aware of the important pieces you might need while being prepared for the worst-case scenarios will allow you to be that warrior in the garden.

Crossroads

There is a powerful internal feeling that comes from facing a crossroads. We make decisions all the time, but when we encounter these pivotal moments, we can truly begin to understand the profound impact that a single decision can have on our lives and how it can change everything for better or worse.

It is crucial to grasp the concept of crossroads. When standing at a physical crossroads, we realize that by not choosing one path, we may never discover what lies down that path. It is important to remind ourselves of this frequently, whether through an image, music, or an object—anything that can serve as a reminder that the daily decisions we make guide us toward the island of freedom, the continent of conformity, or the vast blue ocean of uncertainty.

The idea of the "crossroads" holds spiritual significance, as exemplified by blues musician Robert Johnson in the 1930s. Despite not being recognized as an exceptionally talented musician, Johnson disappeared for several months and returned with a completely unique way of playing his guitar. His lyrics often referenced a crossroads, and some alluded to dark entities that he believed would eventually come for him. Rumors circulated that Johnson had made a deal with the devil at the crossroads in exchange for his fame.

The crossroads have long been known as a place to pray to heaven or sell your soul. Either way, it is most definitely a place to find yourself, and there is great significance in the crossroads as a metaphor for our connection to the world we create through the decisions we make.

How do You Decide

You are standing at a crossroads, and now you understand how important the decision you're about to make will be. We all desire to "have our cake and eat it too," but this book emphasizes realism and understanding. You can't travel down both roads at the same time, and you can't stand there forever thinking about it. Some things are within your control, and some are beyond your control. Here at the crossroads, there's no choice—you have to make a decision, it's beyond your control.

Confidence comes from knowing that you are going to make a decision and knowing how to process that information regarding the direction of your next, and ultimate goals. Understand what you can control and make the best decision for the best outcome. When the time comes that your catalyst has provided you with your freedom, this decision can be made with a coin toss—it won't matter, that's how confident you will be. On the road between this point and that one though, you are sure to come to many crossroads that will require you to stop, remember the lessons you've learned, and make a decision based on the outcome that you desire, your ultimate or most immediate goal. Through the knowledge of your direction of intent and the awareness of the reality of the situation at hand, your crossroads will all eventually begin to lead to the same place.

Define your direction. Where are you going? And why?

Control your emotions. The desire to see what is down the other road may take you from your chosen path.

Perception. Perceive the situation for what it is, not what you wish it to be. What is your next goal and which card will help you move those pieces to those places?

One of these roads will take you to your desired destination fastest, with the smoothest path, and the best weather. If one factor is not ideal, weigh the pros against the cons. The road may be rocky but with good weather, and another may be a smooth road with bad weather. Which road will take you where you intend to go with the most security? The fastest route is not always the best. If it takes more time and patience, you may still arrive at your destination faster than the seemingly fastest path with the rockiest road.

Don't Burn Bridges

Metaphorically speaking, as you travel down the various roads of life, you will encounter other travelers. Share your stories and get to know these fellow travelers; they will impart valuable lessons they have learned, so be sure to listen. *"We have two ears and one mouth so that we can listen twice as much as we speak" - Epictetus*

Maintain those relationships and treat others as you would want to be treated yourself because the day may come when the road you choose becomes too rocky to continue on, and you need to use their bridge for support to find a new way forward. This goes hand in hand with humility, patience, and understanding. When you approach others with passion and care, your efforts will be appreciated, and more opportunities will open up to help you reach your destination.

When you cross a bridge that has been offered to you by one of these relationships, be sure to be present in the moment and humble, understanding that access to this bridge comes from outside sources. Regardless of any contribution you may have made to foster that relationship, recognize that you are utilizing their bridge at that moment. Always strive to reciprocate with something even greater as a gesture of gratitude. It isn't until you look back sometimes that you realize all that you take for granted, so don't make those mistakes. Be appreciative and let it be known.

Where Are You Going?

As you discover who you are and what you want from this life, a natural question will begin to arise from those conversations: "Where do you want to be?" Becoming the person that you want to be for your own reasons may be difficult in the place that you are currently at, surrounded by the people who know you to be the person you used to be. When you try to change yourself, you will most definitely face opposition from those who want you to remain just the way you are because you fit into their narrative. But fitting into their narrative is like working for someone else; you are helping others achieve their dreams without discovering your own.

Don't be the cog in the wheel, be the hub. Create a life that springs forth from your own desires and aspirations, not from someone or something else. How you find the base for your hub should be decided by assessing many factors because it's not a decision to be taken lightly, especially if you are leaving everything you have ever known. Certain places are better than others in terms of quality of life, opportunity, and peace of mind. Your goal is freedom, so start there. Would you be happy to die in the place you have decided to be? Will you have more options in terms of opportunities? Or at least, do the pros outweigh the cons? Most people have talent or skills acquired from training for the occupation they currently have, and a desire for the fruition of the talent they now seek to explore for themselves, and it's okay, perhaps better, if they are one and the same.

So find that place that makes you happy, will allow you to create the life you want for yourself, make you a better person, and ultimately satisfy you when you look back over your life as it comes to an end. If you have taken the time to genuinely discover yourself and you have mapped out what you intend to achieve for happiness in this life, then I promise you, you will know when it's right—you will feel it. If keeping a structured life and sleep pattern gives you control, imagine what the right place does for your state of mental control. It's your place, for your future, for your freedom, because of the decisions that *you* have made.

Obstacles

Success is limited by desire. Make sure to analyze your progress consistently, so you can realize sooner rather than later if you are becoming bogged down or digging a hole. If you are digging a hole, realize that you won't get out unless you stop digging and start climbing. Find peace, find that place you want to create, and do these things for the right reasons because desire is truly the only way to focus on and create what it is that you're seeking.

Imagine the path you have chosen. You know there will be obstacles to overcome, some big and some small.

The day may come when obstacles amount to the size of a mountain, maybe even at the beginning of your path. When you sit and ponder these obstacles and how to get around them, first address what they are. You may find that they are fear, anxiety, frustration, anger, or distrust. These types of obstacles appear to be heavy and hard to move, but as you strive to understand what they are and how they got there in the first place, you'll realize that the same place they come from is the same place that can remove them. They are not heavy, they are perceptions created from thought, that appear to be roadblocks. Perception of thought can also unblock them from your path.

The point is to identify this white noise within you and continuously work to remove anything unnecessary from your mind. This will free up and simplify the true objectives of your path, and amplify the beauty that surrounds it. The more beauty and positivity you see coming from your path, the more ugliness, negativity, and matters of insignificance will be muffled.

Chapter 6

"The Man who says he can, and the man who says he can not... Are both correct"

- Confucius

Time, patience, vision, and experience—everything begins with structure. Just as seedlings start by growing roots and homes start with foundations, you must move pieces to their proper places. If your life feels chaotic, it may simply be because the individual pieces are scattered across your "real estate." Begin by identifying what is part of the foundation, main floor, second floor, roof, etc., and then start moving the pieces to their proper places so construction can begin. Just as a seedling establishes roots for structure before growing, so too must you start building your vision. Begin brainstorming, look for role models in your field, and learn about their beginnings and paths to success. Begin the necessary work to educate yourself and envision the life that you *will* lead.

Where There Is a Will, There Is a Way

Keep this saying close to your heart, because it's true. If you have the will to succeed in the venture that you've set out upon, you will find a way. Remember that we do better because of the desire we have to do so. When times get tough and the road gets rocky, intentional effort for proper reasons will provide a will strong enough to defeat the opposition. Your perception of how things work and why you're doing what you're doing will be the determining factor in your success for freedom.

As I said before, it takes time and patience. Do your best to lessen the time it takes to achieve what you want, but don't get discouraged if you have setbacks along the way. Learn the lessons that will make you stronger, assess the issues and rely on your will to succeed in completing your next goal. Keep your eyes fixated on the prize, like the bird on a wire, and find a way.

Life is like the rapids of a river: you find yourself nervously and frantically swimming against the current out of fear of losing control and being swept away to an uncertain fate. But, just as you would in the actual rapid current of a river, calm yourself, turn yourself around, and let the river take you. Extend your legs for protection and use the current to your advantage as you focus and slowly navigate yourself toward the shore.

The One You Feed

A grandfather is talking with his grandson. The grandfather says, "In life, there are two wolves inside of us that are always at battle. One is a good wolf which represents things like kindness, bravery, and love. The other is a bad wolf which represents things like greed, hatred, and fear." The grandson stops and thinks about it for a second, then he looks up at his grandfather and says, "Grandfather, which one wins?" The grandfather replies, "The one you feed."

People only seem to focus on the micro-environment they are accustomed to for the prospect of safety, so their world exists primarily within that space. As you educate yourself and broaden your wealth of knowledge, you will discover fascinating and amazing things about the world that exists around you: the ocean, forests, space, countries, and cultures. There is so much to learn, see, and do! The more you understand, the smaller and more simplistic everything becomes. Will you let the idea of safety in a carefully controlled environment keep you from experiencing what is available to you?

Determine who you are, what you want, and feed those ideas everything they need to thrive. Coming to a place within yourself that gives you direction and a non-delusional perception, allows you to move freely in the direction of your own desires. If you feel as though life has been filled with negative events, and now at the beginning of your new journey, you deserve to have positivity and everything you want in life to happen, then realize that the events we consider negative and the situations that arise from them are due to personal choices and decisions which put us there in the first place.

Yes, we all deserve to be wealthy, happy, in love, and in the place we want to be. All of these ideas that create the positive environment you feel you deserve will come from keeping an idea that you know what you want, and that the decisions you make will take you there. No one and nothing else is going to *give* it to you. It is your vision, your will, and your decisions that make it so.

Knowledge and Intention

Having a clear and concise vision of what you desire is crucial. Whether it's writing, images, or videos—use whatever method best brings your vision to life. Fully immerse yourself in it, and you'll steadily move toward your goal. The main focus should be on freedom, not just money, though the two often go hand in hand. Achieving a sense of inner peace requires freedom, which in turn often requires financial stability to allow for discovery and self-awareness. In our society, freedom is challenging to achieve without financial means, so think of money as a tool, like a hammer. Just as you need to learn how to wield a hammer to build a house, you need to understand how to use money effectively to build a life of freedom.

you can't be free without the financial means to support your desired lifestyle, without being where you truly want to be, or without moving through life with purpose and intention. Ask yourself, what can you do on the side to generate additional income? What is your annual financial goal based on the lifestyle you envision? What strategies can you implement to reduce your tax burden? Do you take time to understand critical financial concepts like yields, good and bad debt, and interest rates? These are powerful tools designed to help you achieve your goals, but they require proper knowledge and understanding before use.

Most financial situations can trap you in a difficult position if you're not educated on how the system works. Often, these systems are structured to benefit others more than you. For instance, if you deposit a large sum of money in a bank, you might earn a 0.5% yield. Meanwhile, the bank loans that money out at 8% interest, profiting from the 7.5% difference. This practice, known as the interest rate spread, illustrates how different levels of financial knowledge and education can lead to vastly different outcomes and lifestyles. By making informed decisions and continually educating yourself about financial strategies, you maximize your potential for achieving freedom and happiness.

What about all of the white noise? Advertising and sponsorships from our peers are constantly pushed on us. Computers are using classification algorithms to sell us more things that we really don't need. All of this while trying to play the game, and getting just enough to keep supplying the means to continue to destroy the very place we exist, and our minds and freedom with it. Use this equation from the book "*The Millionaire Next Door*" to help you begin to understand the reality of your current situation: *"Multiply your age times your realized pretax annual household income from all sources except inheritances. Divide by ten. This, less any inherited wealth, is what your net worth should be."*

Getting out of the hole you're already in will take time, understanding your purchasing power, leverage, and what you can do to create lump sum infusions of money that have an intended purpose. You have to learn and play the game. Society won't let you be free going against the grain, believe me. Only if you play your own game against them, in the same way, or better than they do, can you reach financial goals. Will it take time? Yes. Is it going to take a lot of knowledge and connections? Yes.

You need to be honest with yourself and acknowledge the situation for what it is. Have you fallen into a bad routine? Are you stuck on the hamster wheel? Procrastination will destroy your progress. Writing down your goals, turning off the television, putting down video games and social media while you go through the list of educational materials to become informed on what to do when you reach your next monetary goal, will get you there faster. Move pieces to places with intention based on a realistic time frame.

What do you intend to do now? When your approach is based on a stronger foundation, a clearer vision, and deeper understanding, free from external distractions, you will be better equipped to determine your next steps in moving forward. There is a saying when referring to gambling: "*Don't play with scared money.*" You move forward wholeheartedly and expect to win, because you're not playing with scared money, unsure if what you're doing is right or wrong, knowing that if you lose, you had already accepted that outcome and planned for it before you even started playing. If the feeling you're getting is one of uncertainty and concern, then you're playing with scared money and you are always going to second-guess your decisions and feel poorly when you don't win.

When you find a concept that inspires you, focus on studying it from different angles. As you gain knowledge and practice, you'll start to understand and know what to expect. Whatever you desire, break it down into smaller parts and focus on the next step. Moving forward with knowledge and intention, with a focus on goals. This will help you climb your ladder faster.

Necessary Changes

You've decided to live a life of freedom and do what's necessary to succeed in getting there. It's challenging to resist joining the crowds, experiencing moments, or using time and money for yourself by buying things and going places. If you want it all, all the time, then you need to start immediately by following through with your vision, gaining knowledge, and moving with intention. These difficulties will subside as you witness your future gradually unfolding before you. Stay focused and let that progress serve as motivation.

Consider concrete: once it's mixed and hits the ground, there's no option to stop midway. You must see it through to completion, or it will be wasted. Approach your life with the same determination. When you were born, the concrete hit the ground. Work with intention like you've never worked before because when your time's up and everything has solidified, you'll either finish with the intended result or see it wasted.

How can you reach a point where you have the financial freedom to break free from conventional thinking and start seeing things from outside the box? For most of us, even after a few weeks of living below our means and saving money, we'll feel the need to reward ourselves. Living below your means requires finding something inexpensive that brings you joy to keep you moving upward toward your goals. Get out of your city or town, and use those moments to expand your perception of nature and your awareness of yourself. Quietly step out of the box and envision the moment when your accomplishments have provided you the freedom to live with peace of mind at all times, not just when escaping to the beauty of nature.

Establish a plan and a budget to grow your wealth to a level that aligns with your aspirations. Whatever you earn, take no less than 10% of it (pre-tax) and prioritize this savings before any other expenses. If you can't save 10%, cut unnecessary expenses, or adjust your living situation to get to that position. Cancel subscriptions you don't use, or seek out different companies that offer similar products at a lower rate. The best way to accomplish this is by "paying yourself first."

I know what you're thinking—10% is not enough. You're right; a consistent 35% would be ideal (20% for savings and 15% for investments). However, starting with 10% is better than nothing. Realizing that 10% isn't enough can be the motivation you need to seek out ways to create a more substantial financial cushion. With even just 10%, you can build a safety net, create products, invest in markets, and develop the habits and mental exercises necessary for wealth creation. Don't think of it as just 10% for years and years; think of it as building a habit for protection while you come up with ways to speed up the process. This would be a good time to read "*The Richest Man in Babylon*" by George S. Clason.

When you receive your pay for traded labor, saving 10% is a good starting point. Take that 10% and give it to yourself first by placing it in a federally insured high-yield savings (HYS) account, rather than a standard 0.5% account. This initial step can be the foundation for building an emergency fund, which will give you peace of mind and financial stability. As you become more consistent with this habit, aim to increase your savings rate to 15%, then 20%, or more. Maximize contributions to a Roth IRA and take advantage of company 401(k) matches. This not only helps you build wealth but also prepares you for unexpected expenses and future opportunities.

When you increase the amounts that go straight to yourself, you'll be motivated to maintain and increase your income, fostering a cycle of growth. As you boost the percentage allocated to your savings, aim to emulate the financial practices of successful investors, gradually building wealth and enhancing your financial security. Do the research and gain the knowledge necessary to use that income to invest in education, ideas, products, or services that increase your return, ultimately achieving a 100% realization of your goals.

The aim is to create a "Plan B"—a financial safety net that allows you to pursue ventures that can eventually free you from the constraints of a complacent lifestyle and the relentless cycle of the hamster wheel. Your goal should be to accumulate enough wealth to support your lifestyle through a sustainable return. For example, accumulating $250,000 at a 5% return could yield $12,500 annually, equating to over $1,000 a month. Doubling this investment could bring you close to the current minimum wage, and further doubling could result in an over $4,000 of monthly income.

Regularly investing $1,000 per month at just a 5% annual percentage yield (APY) could make you a millionaire in 34 years. However, we often realize the importance of financial planning only as we grow older. Strive to improve your financial situation by seeking opportunities for passive income and remaining focused on your goals. Approach wealth-building with a mindset of consistent contribution and seek innovative ways to accelerate your progress.

Those who grasp the importance of investing and leveraging their resources strategically are always looking for ways to invest and make their money work for them. When you have the money, you can allocate your time to these efforts. The wealthy are on a trajectory of exponential growth because ideally, they move the needle daily, while the poor move the needle bi-weekly. If you think the task is too great, you may never get there. If you break it down and ask yourself, "How can I?" you'll be much closer to finding a solution than if you avoid facing the reality of the facts.

Exercise caution when making career decisions. The need to create income sometimes causes us to jump at an opportunity, but rushing into a job out of necessity can lead to regret and dissatisfaction. Take the time to research and find something that makes you happy, pays well, and allows you to start working yourself off the wheel. Explore opportunities that align with your interests, values, and financial goals. Prioritize your well-being and long-term goals by working to learn or seeking fulfilling work that offers financial stability and independence. By staying focused, making informed decisions, and investing in your future, you can break free from the cycle of financial instability. This will allow you to start working yourself off the wheel and build a secure foundation for a fulfilling life.

Exercise

Part of a structured life should include a routine that promotes well-being. In modern times, the necessity and benefits of a hunter-gatherer mindset have diminished, leading to more sedentary and complacent lifestyles. Since the need to physically seek out food and resources is no longer present, we must counteract this sedentary tendency by regularly exercising both the mind and body.

Engage in activities like stretching and exercising that are easily manageable, ensuring consistency. Remember, a gym membership is only beneficial if you use it. If you become discouraged and criticize yourself for not going or for wasting money on something unused, it can have a negative impact. Physical education (P.E.) in schools has always emphasized the importance of exercise. However, when people think about working out, they often imagine going to the gym, lifting weights, or running—activities that can feel overwhelming and discourage them from exercising, ultimately resulting in the opposite of the intended effect.

Find manageable activities like Tai Chi, Yoga, or other stretching exercises that are simple to incorporate into daily life. These practices don't have to consume your day. They typically involve stretching your legs, back, arms, etc. Including activities like calisthenics—simple bodyweight exercises such as push-ups, squats, lunges, and sit-ups—doesn't require special equipment and can be done anywhere, making them an excellent way to get your blood flowing, boost energy, limber muscles, and stimulate the mind.

If the path you choose involves either building muscle mass or achieving the flexibility of dance, it's important to learn what works best for that particular goal. Just know that skipping a "workout" can be more detrimental to your health than simply stretching and doing some jumping jacks in the morning. These exercises can be a brief part of your day using items you already have, such as a couch, doorway, or chair. Establishing a daily routine like this can help you feel better, gain focus, and continue with your day.

A well-structured morning routine can also lead to increased productivity and a sense of accomplishment. Morning routines may include activities such as making the bed, enjoying a quiet moment with coffee, reading the news, stretching, exercising, eating a healthy breakfast, reading a chapter of a book, meditating, journaling, solving puzzles, playing a card game, or studying a new language. These can all contribute to a balanced and fulfilling start to the day. Breaking these activities into small, manageable steps makes them easier to incorporate into daily life, promoting consistency.

By organizing a variety of tasks in a sequence, it's possible to move through the routine quickly and seamlessly. Knowing how long each task will take and having a clear plan for what comes next minimizes wasted time, fostering a smoother and more efficient flow. This approach also helps buffer against external pressures, enhancing personal well-being and maintaining productivity.

Maintaining a positive mindset can significantly influence how the day unfolds. Even on days when waking up with less than optimal amounts of sleep, having the determination to stick to a structured routine can be a way of asserting control over the day, regardless of external circumstances. If you think, "I didn't get a full night's rest, I'm going to be tired" then guess what? you'll become tired. The mentality of your control on the day is what makes an alarm an abstract thing. It's what makes the weather a beautiful and uncontrollable force. It's what makes the attitude of individuals ineffective to yours in any way you consider detrimental.

Chapter 7

"The fear of death follows from the fear of life. A man who lives fully is prepared to die at any time."
― *Mark Twain*

Life's greatest moments, and the most intense energies that you will feel, come from things that are dangerous to some degree or another. It's in that confrontation with mortality that gives us the adrenaline rush, causing a deeper sense of meaning and the realization of fragility. We need these moments if we want to feel alive.

Open yourself up to the deepest sense of awareness. Look deeply at everything you can, study it, and try to understand it until you can *feel* it! The tree you sit under may have existed since before your grandparents. The beach you walk on took millions of years to grind rock into small grains of sand. The mountains you hike or drive through were created by massive collisions of the earth's crust or the explosion of multiple volcanoes that destroyed everything you see for thousands of years. You can't fully grasp these ideas without experiencing them, trying to understand them, and experiencing a deep humility because of them.

Fear and Death

It's fear. Fear of failure, fear of exposure, fear of dying, and the unknown. There are moments where you must conquer fear because what you desire is on the other side of it. Everyone knows that person who seems to surround themselves with drama, who can never seem to get things in order, or always has something they are dealing with. Most people have addictions, habits, projects, drama, or disorganization. Why do we distract ourselves so much?

For a moment, consider what you might want to distract yourself from the most. What would be any human being's biggest fear? Fear of the unknown? Fear of uncertainty? It's the fear of death. We all fear death because it is ever-present, capable of striking at any moment, and shrouded in uncertainty. We all believe in something, but no matter how much faith we have, the day of reckoning will come when we die.

What about the fear of failure? Or the fear of being exposed to your peers for who you truly are? On all levels of consciousness, the fear of death is relevant and can manifest in subtle ways, influencing behaviors, beliefs, and emotions without individuals being fully aware of it. The fear of death can shape one's attitudes toward risk-taking, relationships, and the pursuit of goals. This awareness instills a constant internal anxiety and fear, leading us to create distractions. For some, there is a level of frustration that comes from being afraid and not in control; hurting people, animals, or even seeking positions of power for the feeling of control because it makes the individual feel better about themselves or their own situation in comparison. However, most of us are content to run in the maze, chasing after the cheese, because it gives us something to focus on.

Death is an unchangeable and constant part of life. Understanding and facing these fears is necessary for awareness. These harsh realities are for you to begin to see that every day, some dramatics, some project, a movie, a night out drinking, these are distractions that we surround ourselves with. Time moves faster and faster. Ironically, as we distract ourselves, we inadvertently hasten its arrival. And when that day does come, we may find ourselves thinking, "But there's so much I haven't done! I'm not ready." When you accept your fate, and understand your fleeting moment on this earth, *then* you can begin to live.

How can you prepare yourself to look death in the eyes when it comes and say with a calm mind and a steady hand "I'm ready"? Like many things outlined in this book, the concept is to begin to understand, accept, and deal with the issues first by looking directly at them, stripping away the white noise, and seeing them for what they truly are. Now, I can't give you the complete understanding of what is going to happen to you when you die, or when that will take place (nobody can), but I can describe to you an Idea that may help you to at least accept it, so that you can get busy enjoying this life, freely, instead of distracting yourself from it. *"Life can only be understood backwards; but it must be lived forwards." - Soren Kierkegaard*

Perception is the key to everything, the flip side of the coin. Take a piece of material, any material, and observe it closely with the naked eye. You'll see what you as an organism need to see, to be able to interpret it within your environment. Now put it under a microscope and magnify it x100, it becomes something different, and again x1000, it becomes something else entirely. There is much more going on around you than you could ever fathom. Amplifying your awareness helps you to better realize these insights, but to what end? That *you* are also comprised of a trillion cells, each containing around 100 trillion atoms. We once believed the atom to be the base of all things, but we now know that atoms can be divided into protons, neutrons, and electrons, which are made of even smaller particles called quarks.

The point here is to understand that individuals grasping at life understand very little of the larger picture, due to the distractions that are deemed to have much more importance. It would be in our best interest to experience life more openly, and deeply. Project yourself to the end of your life, what do you want it to be? What do you want to have accomplished? Go to that place now and follow the ideas laid out at the beginning of this book to idealize what you want from the life you have, in the amount of time you might have to accomplish it.

The doctor in the movie tells the patient they have two weeks to live—how suspenseful! It's an escape from our own lives to get caught up in that drama, but put yourself in that patient's shoes. What if the doctor gave you only two weeks to live? Imagine it realistically and seriously, and ask yourself, "What do I need to have in my life to accept those outcomes?"

Psychiatrist Elisabeth Kubler-Ross wrote the seminal book *On Death and Dying* in the '60s, based on her groundbreaking work with terminally ill patients. In it, she outlined the five stages of grief:

1. **Denial**: 'It can't be true' or 'This can't be happening to me.'
2. **Anger**: 'But there's so much I haven't done! I'm not ready.'
3. **Bargaining**: 'Please just give me one more chance (more time).'
4. **Depression**: Pushing loved ones away or retreating into a shell.
5. **Acceptance**: Telling loved ones that 'everything will be okay' and expressing love.

I have personally witnessed the incredible transformation that can occur when a person is facing death, in terms of acceptance and the emotions surrounding life when faced with limited time. "*I want to see as much as possible*," she said to me. Ideally, we would all experience these stages if we had enough time at the end of our lives. So, what I suggest is to imagine this scenario now in your mind.

This deeply personal journey involves confronting existential questions, finding meaning and purpose in life, and embracing the reality of mortality with courage and acceptance. In this way, you can face fears, reduce anxieties, and begin to see more clearly. You can envision yourself in a place where you can say, "I accepted this moment years ago. Not only did I accept it, but I expected it at any moment, and I have lived my life to the fullest, doing what I wanted." As Marcus Aurelius said, "*Think of yourself as dead. You have lived your life. Now, take what's left and live it properly.*"

Health, Wealth, Love, and Environment

Your freedom is acquired through awareness, but happiness will come in the form of these four things:

Health. Having good health allows you to take steps toward maintaining a healthy mind and body. Physical exercise, as discussed in Chapter 6, does not have to be done in a perfect setting or resemble what is seen on TV or the internet. A form of meditation is also beneficial for everyone, even though not everyone may be comfortable with it or feel that it works for them. However, many do not realize that meditation is meant to quiet the mind and improve focus, which can be achieved through activities like jogging, playing cards, or reading (which is also a great way to exercise the mind and educate yourself at the same time).

Wealth. Accumulating wealth gives you more control over your life. Building structured systems that implement calculated moves, instead of squandering funds, helps train the mind to focus more on needs than wants. For instance, a morning routine would never *have* to change with outside influences like money; it's a form of discipline, completely unrelated to wealth. Wealth is important for protection and freedom in this world, but it should not define one's identity; it should be viewed as a tool. A millionaire who is unhappy is not truly successful.

Love. Love is the one thing that has so many variables beyond your control. It is very important, but it is also very important that you know who you are and what you want before you try to share that with someone else. The right person can make you and the wrong one can break you.

Environment. Lastly, your environment plays a significant role in your happiness. Feeling content and free in your surroundings can reduce distractions and help you focus on forming connections and pursuing your goals with ease and comfort.

Knowing Yourself

Leaders lead by example and motivate through confidence that comes from knowledge and focus. Respect must be given and earned before it can be received, and trust can take a long time to develop but only an instant to destroy. Educate yourself on the needs of those around you, be available to offer support without expectations, and you will find that one of the best feelings in the world is having that support returned to you in full force as you move forward—not alone, but as a united front.

When asking the question, "Who am I?" be sure to include all the little details. When you look back time and time again, it will help paint a broader picture of yourself. What brings you joy is part of who you are. What you like to wear, your favorite seasons or holidays, your best talents, or your favorite kind of work all contribute to your identity. You are sharing these things with yourself, for yourself, not for anyone else, so being honest with yourself is crucial if you want to truly explore the ideas that will set your spirit free.

Another question worth considering is: if you understand what needs to change, why not take the necessary steps to improve yourself? You know what you like and dislike, as well as what is good for you and what is not. If you encounter something you don't like or know is harmful to you, then how can you take steps to change it? Or, why *aren't* you taking steps to change it?

Plan and Detail

What a great feeling it is to know what you desire, who you want to be as a person, and that as that person you are untouchable, by fear and even death. You are in pursuit of purity, humility, simplicity as well as a true understanding and acceptance of what you cannot control, but saying it and being it are two different things. You have to transition somehow from who and where you are now to who and where you want to be. Take as much time as necessary to take it one step at a time. For the first step to be 100% positive and confident in what you have described as your ideal scenario, make sure it has been pondered, considered, criticized by you, and reaffirmed to be true. This is a crossroads, so make sure to define your direction.

Where are you going? And why? Control your emotions and perceive the situation for what it is, not what you wish it to be. Additionally, utilize visual aids such as pictures or a vision board to help you imagine and dream about the concepts you've been developing. If these visuals lift your spirit, and you become more and more excited about the prospect of them, then you will know that you're on the right path. Once you know that you are on the right path, you can begin to research and plan in detail what it would take to begin to execute those plans and bring them to fruition. Through research and development, you will be able to adjust your smaller steps in relation to the next goal. Continue to self-check daily that you are becoming excited by the prospect of them, knowing without a doubt that your course is the right one for you.

Be aware that when you complete that final goal, it's not a stopping point. Think about what you would like to do *after* completing your goals. Just as we strive to become educated to accomplish our goals, we will continue to push, on our own terms, to do the things that have inspired us to be children again.

The structure you create is the determining factor between being lost and experiencing life. It serves as a guide to explore, a source of motivation, and something to keep you moving forward. It's all a game, a perception of one's reality, created by a subconscious mind with a pre-set condition of how things should be. It's time to take back control, to dive deep and change the software that creates the game so that you can begin to take control of the narrative and where the story goes.

Study and Execute

At this stage, you should become excited, excited enough and inspired enough, to get to work. You've spoken it, envisioned it, detailed how it will go, and planned your next steps. So now, what details are missing? When you come to a body of water with the intention to go swimming, you don't just jump in. You enter slowly to assess the temperature, or ask someone who is already in the water for the information you need before jumping in, so that you can mentally prepare yourself.

Consider this concept: if a person could go back in time, what would they tell themselves? What would they try to convey to others? Typically, a person goes through life making mistakes, learning, and wishing they could change something. As they age, they try to impart these lessons to younger generations, but as human beings, we tend to want to learn on our own and are ingrained with those unconscious teachings from our youth.

If you consider this for a moment, and instead of living your life and then trying to mentor someone who doesn't believe that your opinion is relevant to their generation, take it upon yourself to have conversations with older generations and individuals with experience in your desired direction. You'll find that many of life's common mistakes, which take away the little time you have in this life, have been experienced by others who are willing to share concepts of what not to do or what they would change if they had the chance. This is valuable knowledge that you can carry with you as you move forward.

The Chinese philosopher Confucius emphasized that learning through imitation—essentially from others' experiences—is the simplest and least painful way to gain wisdom. Personal experience, while valuable, is often harsh and unnecessary when you can learn from others. *"By three methods we may learn wisdom: First, by reflection, which is noblest; second, by imitation, which is easiest; and third by experience, which is the bitterest."*

Once you've studied to find the missing details, mentally prepared yourself, and found mentors to give you guidance and insight, you will be confident enough to take the first step toward achieving your next goal. Execute your plan with precision, patience, and foresight. Confidence comes from visualizing the steps in your mind toward each goal, leading to the main goal you have set for yourself.

By executing this plan, you'll know the details: what should happen, what is happening, what the variables are, and what the exit strategy is. Make sure to continue motivating yourself and constantly checking your work against your plan. This approach addresses issues before they become problems and prepares you to mentor others by passing along valuable information.

Chapter 8

"A man is but the product of his thoughts. What he thinks, he becomes."

- Mahatma Gandhi

Without even realizing it, just by reading up to this point, your subconscious has absorbed and stored information. Your subconscious mind holds a concept that the unconscious mind lacks the necessary information for achieving your ultimate goals. It understands that it is the most powerful part of the mind, but often defers decision-making to a faulty foundation that lacks a solid basis. Now, your subconscious is beginning to recognize the need to take control and guide the conscious mind toward a more solid and purposeful direction.

Your subconscious knows that for you to become the best person you can be, you're going to have to restructure that foundation into a very simple, but strong, foundation of self, which should revolve around a basis of you—not your parents or grandparents—and involves understanding who you are, what you want, and where you want to be. These are the fundamental pieces that will create your new foundation. That foundation is being built on real estate of basic principles that already exist, the positive educational influences from your past. And now educational theory exists within the subconscious to implement ideas of awareness, individual freedom, manifestation, education, patience, structure, intention, and humility.

Everything you desire begins with taking the first step—a foot in the door leading to a long hallway filled with doors on either side, and one at the end. The door at the end of the hallway leads to your next goal. But can you stay focused and pass by all the other doors? Getting that first step in the door is challenging, and I've written this book because I've faced those challenges all the way down the hall. Each time, I felt the pain of loss in time, relationships, money, or other factors as I explored many doors out of curiosity. When I finally reached the door at the end and looked back at all the paths that led nowhere, I realized the importance of focusing on the right door. I wanted to share this insight with others, advising them not to waste effort on opening every door, but to remain focused on the door that truly matters.

Just like planting a fruit tree, you can't go out the next day and collect the fruit. The steps that you will take now to plant the tree will take time to bear that fruit. Don't become distracted and impatient that it hasn't yielded anything overnight, instead, continue to water and take care of it. If you walk away, distracted by something else, it may die, or bear fruit when you are not around to benefit. Fruition is achieved through goals, steps, and actions.

It comes down to the simple and basic principles of diligence, patience, and time. How much wealth do you need? If you break it down into years plus compounded interest, then how many years will it take? How many months? How much is that in a daily contribution? Have fun with these questions until you realize that small steps really do complete large goals, financial or otherwise. If the journey seems daunting, remember that reaching your goals begins by just taking that first step. Don't let your dreams drift away by not starting down that hallway toward the door of success.

Kung Fu 功夫

Routines can start with something small and as you persist in doing them every day, you become more efficient and skilled at them. I've described in this book that knowledge of a particular thing and understanding your perception of it are the keys to answering the questions you have for guidance on your journey. What does Kung Fu mean, and how is it related? Most would simply say that it is a "martial art," but there is a much deeper meaning and philosophical concept that can educate and inspire those who are open to grasping it.

Kung Fu started as a means of exercise and stretching coupled with spiritual healing. All of these are beneficial on your journey, but the main point is what the term itself stands for. Kung Fu roughly means "skill" or "acquired skill." The idealism is to create a process, become educated on proper technique, develop and practice consistently and constantly in dedication to achieve perfection. This gives you a constant in life because perfection never comes; there is no stopping point. There is always something that can be better understood, a better way to perform or portray, and the practice itself is a part of the art being perfected.

So, why Kung Fu? Because it represents so well the ideas of discovery, implementation, practice, patience, skill, and persistence to perfection. The idea itself is as inspiring as a piece of art, music, or object in yours, or anyone's need for inspiration for battling something within that cannot be seen.

Whatever you decide to do, latch on to it, do it 100% all the way. With intention, focus, diligence, and confidence, knowing that once it has been achieved in its basic principles, you will continue to strive to make it better, focusing on all the little details and always trying to perfect it. That's the concept of Kung Fu. The more that you try to understand something, the more you go over and over it, the simpler it becomes. Focus on the stages, continue to grow, and make time for education.

Rome Wasn't Built in a Day

An idea like the last one I described takes a lifetime of practice and execution to develop, so it's important to remember the adage "Rome wasn't built in a day." How many times do you suppose the word "patience" is used in this book? There's a reason. To be patient is very difficult, especially in a fast-food world, but to achieve something by managing it one step at a time and understanding when 20% luck opportunities are in your favor, the rest comes down to how well you can get educated, cover the angles, keep vigilant, and be patient because processes take time.

If you plan to accomplish something in one year, then strive to accomplish it in that year. You need a goal to shoot for. If it takes two, then be honest with your failings and adjust, but don't lose sight of the goal. The formula for fruition is consistency over time. Don't forget to remind yourself that to be great, like Ancient Rome, takes time.

Time is relative. A day can seem so short that you feel as though very little has been accomplished, or you can have a day where you've accomplished a lot, which feels like a long day. If you fill your days intentionally, every day will be a productive and long day. Being a mouse in the maze of society is very difficult. You work, receive your pay, and feel that it should be at least twice that much if you hope to have a decent life and retire, so you work twice as hard and give up more of your time, or sacrifice comforts of being alive in such a vibrant time in human history.

None of it is fair. You should be able to exist in society as your own person with hopes and dreams and have every possible road to opportunities available for you to take. Is it overpopulation? Demand? Greed? Either you'll be a victim of it, or you'll make the moves to seize control. Do you want to live that way forever? As a victim? Of course not. Doesn't that motivate you to succeed then? Some might say, "Not really." But why? Why are people so depressed in these times? The only likely answer seems to be: "Why wouldn't you be?" *"The things you can see, with even a single open eye. It's no wonder that people want to stay blind." - Jordan Peterson*

What a sad story we're writing for ourselves, and have been for so long. Is that humanity? Try to remember that depression stems from things we dwell on. Look ahead to a better time and move forward one day at a time. Go over what you've done and when you look back, it should only be to say "I was there, I've done this and that, and now I'm here and this is the next step." Keep moving. Looking toward the dream that will be. In doing so, you can begin to remove yourself from the horrible reality that everyone else is in. You're different, because of the knowledge you now have about what the situation is, where it's headed, and that you won't be a part of it forever. It won't be hopeless if you're hopeful.

You have lessened the amount of white noise and distraction in your life, so you don't need a TV or video games, and now you have moments when you feel bored. Begin to outline a list of your goals, and fill it out with all the goals you wish to complete, the time frames in which they could be completed, which goal you're on now, and what you need to do to get to the next one. How can you have so much to do and still be bored? Have you been self-checking to ensure you are moving forward? Is your goal clear? Do you have a timeline for it? What about a motivating image of what it is? Have you protected yourself from outside forces that could affect your momentum?

The more you focus on something the closer it will become to being finished. Other things will be sacrificed. Let's hope for the most part that it's just TV, entertainment, or time of self-pity that causes depression. You have an entire list of things to do to take you to the next step. Take care of what must be taken care of in your life and then put all (or as much) of your focus as you can on moving the needle in your favor.

Many of us have bouts of depression, loss of motivation, anger, consumption, or isolation. Horrible feelings that are very difficult to escape from, but it can be done. You just need something that can motivate and drive you. Take that first step to get started, or get away from your isolation. Go camping or hiking, go for a drive, discover something, and take a deep breath. Then, make a plan for what you'll do when you get back that you will persist on until it's accomplished.

Days are like pennies. They don't seem to have much value if you waste one, but a handful of pennies make a dollar and a handful of dollars... and so on. The day comes when your pennies are equal to hundreds of dollars, and you can't remember them even equaling up to one. So don't waste your pennies, give each one a little bit of value and they'll add up before you know it.

Skin in the Game

As with many things, we become inspired, and for a week or so, we get really motivated. Then we start to implement ideas and change our lifestyle. Like I said before, we do better through inspiration. However, there are two factors that you must be aware of: "Fear" and your amount of "Skin in the Game." This is why we need patience—baby steps. If you try to force change too quickly, it won't be long before the mind reverts back to its training.

As we learned in Chapter 2, changing behavioral patterns is not something you can do overnight. It's something you have to tell yourself night after night, making small changes that you will have to force into existence. Then, remind yourself night after night why you are doing them until it becomes natural. That's how we *feel* it happening. You can't see what's happening behind the scenes; all you can do is understand, take the steps, and know that when you feel it's becoming easier, it's working.

Anyone would be afraid to go against the grain, and it's that fear that makes it easier to revert back to old behaviors. It's a sense of safety. Remember that this is the unconscious mind at work. Understanding it helps you and your subconscious overcome it, but it is difficult. What are the basic principles that we have covered so far that can help with this aspect of resistance to forward momentum?

Adversity: Your desires to reach your goals *must* be stronger than your fears.
Intelligence: Understanding when and why you're reverting, so you can act to stop it.
Perception and Emotion: Control your emotions. What you feel has nothing to do with the present moment, but everything to do with how you perceive the future and events that have not yet happened.

If you truly desire something, you must be willing to make a trade for it, plain and simple. Whether you call it karma, Yin & Yang, positive/negative, good and evil, or anything else, just know that the scales must balance in some way. Even if you don't believe that, consider that the mere concept of it gives you humility and grace, not expecting to get without giving. You *are* playing a game, and what is your skin in the game? It's everything—your life! Invest in something to learn. Pay someone for their knowledge, or work to learn. Offer knowledge or work in exchange for assistance, but place your wager because you can't win if you don't play.

I know too well about having skin in the game; whenever I open a door, I bet it all. But that's not what I want for you. I want you to understand where you're going, understand the game and the odds, and place a calculated, hedged bet. That's what winners do. Winners are either taught or they learn.

The Monkey Mind

We fear what we don't know, can't understand, or don't see, but a real fear should be "The Monkey Mind." The monkey mind is what many of us experience when we open other doors and try things that inspire us for a moment but drag us off our path, like a monkey swinging from branch to branch. Your mind becomes unsettled, constantly reaching out to create something instead of living in the present and observing things as they are. Perception is the key. You need steps and goals, similar to moving from branch to branch, but it's the goal that matters. The monkey mind refers to chaotic direction, grabbing at the next thing that seems interesting instead of moving decisively.

Although you may be inspired by many things, you need to write all of them down to see which ones you can do as a hobby, or which ones, being more heavily focused on, can provide you with a better life. Organize these concepts in a linear pattern, so you can focus on them one at a time, you'll find that if you can do one without distraction and create something from it, it will open the door to the next one and so on. This is the domino effect referred to in Chapter 4—"One Card Can Change the Game." If you don't do this, you'll find that you become motivated by different things at different times, and they will pull you in different directions (like the many doors in the hallway). Don't give up on those motivations. Write them down and fit them into a separate category knowing which one demands higher focus for your future, but stick to the next progressive step of what you're currently working on and the time frames you've created for it.

If you can focus your mind clearly on one direction, you're on the right path. If your mind is filled with too many thoughts to focus, that's the monkey mind. Freeing yourself from it requires time and persistence. Organize your priorities by importance and create lists to mark tasks off as you complete them. Relieve yourself of the burden that holding too many tasks in your head can bring. When you still your mind and focus primarily on one thing that will move you up the next step toward achieving your larger goal, direction and motivation are more easily established.

If you find that a particular item never seems to receive a checkmark, there may be some underlying fear associated with it. Confront that fear and complete the task, as it is more crucial than you realize. The *limbic system* and the *nervous system* of the brain and body are internal systems that generate and regulate anxiety. By tackling and conquering challenges like these, you demonstrate to these systems that you are capable of overcoming fear rather than succumbing to perceived danger. With focused effort, you will often find that achieving the task doesn't require much time or energy; there is simply an internal barrier preventing you from doing it.

Other items should be categorized on one side of the path or the other. They are either unnecessary and should be disregarded, or they are issues/situations that need to be addressed. Prioritize anything of utmost importance and incorporate it into your immediate goals. If it is not a top priority, place it slightly off the path, set a timeline for handling it, and concentrate on the primary objectives first.

Aim for the Middle

If you want something you're going to have to pay for it. Think of it as a trade. If you don't get what you thought you wanted, there's a reason. Either you didn't really want it, or you needed to trade it for something else. Maybe that path leads to something bad for you, even though you thought it would be the best thing in the world. This is in reference to a balance theory, like the symbolism of Yin & Yang.

The Middle Way emphasizes finding balance in all aspects of life, avoiding extremes of excess and deficiency, and cultivating wisdom and compassion. As you move along your chosen path there will be swings of positive and negative, good times and bad times. The funny part is that your perception of what is bad could be saving you and you'll just never know it. What seems to be something good could also develop into a nightmare. Work hard in trade for your goals. When you have all you desire and more, walk the path of oneness in the middle way, offer something in return for anything excessive to help yourself remain humble.

I stated earlier in the book that if you look hard enough and interpret the meaning of different texts by repetition or example, you will see similar concepts develop. Create your path. It's a constant, a vision of the future. If you were a Hindu in 1,000 B.C., you might follow your "Dharma." As a Buddhist in 500 B.C., you would follow your "Magga." If you were a Taoist in Asia 100 years later, you'd follow the Tao. A Roman or Greek in 400 B.C. could follow their "Logos" (universal divine reason). In Christianity, the "path of righteousness" is also referred to as "Logos" (the way, the word of God). In Judaism in 20 B.C., it's "Logos Endiathetos" (the word remaining within). *"Listening not to me but to the Logos it is wise to agree that all things are one." -Heraclitus (Fragment 50)*

Your path in life is your direction and your reason for being. Live well, treat yourself and others well, and do what makes you happy while respecting what gives you the ability to do so. Your path allows you to really *feel* the sun, hear the birds, smell the moisture in the air or feel the earth. You don't need much, and you don't expect much. Any description of a path is the "middle way," the best way to keep the positive and negative swings within a range that allows your life to flow as a wave moves through the ocean.

Don't expect much and allow yourself time to live with the "scantiest fare," your food will taste better, and every little thing will become more significant through the idea of simplicity. Minimize life's delusions and it will help you to create a quiet mind by reducing the noise. Play the game with an expectation for the middle ground. If you do better, you will be happy and humble with that, while at the same time if you don't do as well, it won't be such a dramatic loss.

How do you experience life and protect yourself from damaging the one piece of real estate you have? How can you be careful without being so cautious that you miss out on the simple pleasures of life? Aim for the middle. Find the balance between your desire to do something constructive and the temptation to engage in something destructive. This is why humility is emphasized in this book. Humility will help you manage yourself if you get more than you need. There is also a focus on intention, perseverance, and goals. They will help you elevate your efforts if you have less than you need. If you manage your life this way, with your desired goal in mind, you can strive to achieve what you want without over-leveraging yourself or living in fear. Along the way, as you create your desired outcome, aiming for balance will allow you to meet people and build relationships that will be available to you when you need them, and respect you even when you don't.

We know that there are many people who have more than they need. I imagine it must be very difficult for them to live the life that I am describing in this text. If you don't have money, you're not free. Yet, if you are consumed by money, you're not free either. Be mindful of that. What is it that you desire? Will you seek the middle way? The way that allows you to live freely with knowledge and experience of oneness, without the constant bombardment of society, never allowing you to be free, only "money rich."

Even the King, Alexander the Great was known for saying: *"When you bury my body, keep my hands outside so the world knows that the person who conquered the whole world had nothing in their hands while dying."* If all of humankind could see and understand this example from outside of the box, then we as a whole would know that we have gained much more than we have given, in respect to that oneness. Without living the middle way, we will continue to take more and more until balance comes, just as the shore comes to break the wave.

Chapter 9

"There are two things a person should never be angry at: What they can help, and what they cannot."

- Plato

The following sections outline key factors to consider when developing your ideas. Hopefully, they will inspire you to a broader awareness of your surroundings and the future possibilities that lie ahead. *"You must dive into the depths of your own soul, shut out the world and deprive yourself of pleasures. Through this barrage of suffering, life becomes simple and beautiful due to the knowledge of what it is to be without"* - Carl Jung

What could you become if you were given, or if you created, the right circumstances for change? A future directed, dictated, and desired by yourself for a growth larger than that of worldly possessions, but for mastery of the soul.

Food for Thought

Why, what, where, when, who, and how? Answer these questions wholeheartedly with the purpose of understanding yourself and your life's goals, using the knowledge you have acquired from this book.

You need direction first, and then you'll be able to begin. Structure these goals and definitions in a linear pattern like a business model. This is a good way (just as a business model would be) for you to refresh the memory of your intent often, and to remember why you began in the first place. A way to help you check yourself against your own progress, and to pivot as the nature of the world changes. Here is an opportunity for you to take another small step in your journey.

Summary or Mission Statement: What do you hope to achieve in this life? What will make you happy? What will drive you on with vigor? Your "mission statement" is the answer to the question of what it is that you want.

_____

_____

_____

_____

Description: Who are you? Yes, your observations, tutelage, and feelings based on observations of what you consider to be your peers, are shaping who you currently are, but is it really who *you* are? Ask that question, who is behind the mask? Or do you wear no masks? Can you truly be free that way, or is it the expression you mirror from input that you have deemed necessary for acceptance that makes you feel comfortable?

_____

_____

_____

_____

_____

Products and Services: What would you create? What would, or could you do to make the world a better place? What would make you excited to discover? How would you potentially leave a positive mark on the world?

_____

_____

_____

_____

Market Analysis: Are the concepts, goals, services, or creations something that there is a market for? Do people need, or can others potentially benefit from what you're offering to create or do for them? Remember "Expectations of Others" when confiding in friends and family for advice. It's sometimes better to move forward with a concept on your own, to see if you would personally like to pursue it until you're confident and proud enough to handle critique and criticism.

_____

_____

_____

_____

Strategy and Implementation: Steps to goals become goals themselves. What step are you on? What is your highest goal now? Where would you need to be to know that you are financially free? Where are you on that list right now? Will you be in control of your life's direction?

_____

_____

_____

_____

Organization and Management: What players do you need to be involved in your game? Who can help you get to where you want to be? Will the world be better because of what you offer? Do the potential coaches and players in this game feel as passionate as you do about it?

_____

_____

_____

_____

_____

Financial Projections: What is the real potential of what you offer in terms of trade? How many products or services will it take for you to reach your weekly, monthly, or long-term goal? What are the time frames necessary to achieve each individual goal?

_____

_____

_____

_____

_____

The Shift

For us to even exist in this place, everything has to be perfect. Billions of years of moving parts suddenly create a split-second moment in time where we can exist. Humankind is now searching the abyss of space for any sign of life, and yet, even though we're surrounded by the magnificence of life here on Earth, we take it for granted. I can have conscious thoughts and share them with you, and that's amazing!

What does it mean to shift? Evolution in animal characteristics has created some amazing things, and this takes thousands of years to accomplish. Just as a day, relative to a week, a year, several years, and so on, is only a very small part of the "big picture." Another example would be that we see our own faces every day but don't truly grasp the aging process until we refer to images from a long time ago. We are focused on one small moment in time, none of us fully grasp the concept of billions of years of evolution, from the planet's existence to beings, etc. We live in our own little world, in our own little moment in time, and think that everything is about us. How egotistical is that?

Change is happening, and has been happening. Just as a jolt to the system (a catalyst) causes one to look outside the box for answers, a catalyst to the whole system causes a mass of people to start looking outside of the box. This creates the potentiality for evolutionary change, something that is still hard to see in the mirror day-to-day, but it has most definitely begun to happen.

In the 60s, there was a mass movement of love and freedom, a chance to change it all. "We" touched the idea for a moment. Back then they were less dependent and more trusting of one another than we are today, and even they failed to change the human narrative. You can still feel the energy from those that were a part of that moment in time because a piece of it has stayed with them. It's important to discover this place primarily in a natural way so that it can't be lost again. When the majority live in that mentality while being a part of society, we will affect change and inspire others as well.

In my own life, I have looked for answers and truth, and what I have found will affect me for the rest of my life in the way that I live it. The same thing is happening to millions of individuals who also will never be the same, in a good way. We will all inspire and teach one another, with positive energy, and the motivation to gain control of our own lives. Things are changing.

Conscious human beings, constantly observing and learning, naturally advance through time. Significant medical, scientific, and astronomical discoveries often happen within a decade or two. The additional free time afforded by the pandemic has allowed people to step outside of the box. So, what do you do with this excess time? You don't just do the work your job requires of you; instead, you pick up a new hobby, revisit an old one, or start learning something that truly interests you.

Throughout this process, we have made a shift. This is not a temporary condition; it is a direct result of access to one of the pieces of the puzzle, catalyst No. 2: "to be free to do anything and go anywhere." Think of the Renaissance period of the 14th to 17th centuries. Growing out of the Dark Ages, the Crusades, and the Black Plague—great works of art and literature, discoveries in science, medicine, and philosophy were created and discovered, which live on to this day.

The ones that have looked outside the box will find new ways to exist and create change, transforming humankind. If you're reading this, you may be seeking answers, more definitions related to the feelings that have only recently come to you. This shift has begun, raising many questions. This book aims to smooth out the uncertainties and provide a starting point for creating consistency amidst change. By understanding what is happening, we can enhance this beautiful progression, strengthen our self-awareness, and create our own reasons for existing, taking control of our happiness, love, and freedom.

Experiencing a mind-expanding state and describing it is a universal journey we all share, regardless of who we are, when we live, our faith, or our path. We ultimately reach the same beautiful understanding and sense of oneness. Using drugs to reach this state implies a lack of natural methods to achieve it. Relying on drugs can lead to a constant search for the high. Instead, integrate consistent effort, ethical living, and deep contemplation into daily life. Approach this path with patience, dedication, and a compassionate heart, and you will find what you seek, as we all do in time.

Exponential Technological Advancements

The amount of information available to everyone is incredible, perhaps even a little overwhelming. A computer once filled an entire 800-square-foot room 70 years ago. Forty years later, a computer sat on a desktop, and now, 30 years after that, computer devices smaller than grains of rice can be built, and we are standing at the precipice of artificial intelligence.

Exponential growth refers to an increase that occurs at a constant rate per unit of time, leading to a rapid escalation in the quantity over time. For example, 2 becomes 4, then 8, 16, 32, 64, 128, 256, and so on. When a form of technology is discovered, it opens other doors of discovery, leading to more advancements. As people continue to grow and learn about technology, more minds are able to create, opening up even more opportunities for advancement. This exponential technological growth shows no signs of slowing down.

The power that these advancements offer is massive to those who can harness it. Younger generations can process information related to computing and technology on a larger scale than previous generations, leveling the playing field somewhat. However, it is the positions of power that are creating technological advances for purposes of protection and war that are not immediately accessible to the public. What current uses of technology may already exist, and how much longer do we have before the benefits or drawbacks of the exponential growth of these advancements become clear?

The benefits of these advancements include enhanced learning and quick access to information, breaking the distance barrier and enabling remote work or communication with people around the world. This has led to advances in healthcare that have saved lives and increased life expectancy. Our lives are made easier by simplifying tasks, and we are surrounded by entertainment made possible by these advancements.

However, some disadvantages include misinformation and privacy issues. We often receive information that we believe to be true, which can manipulate specific situations. By the time the truth is revealed, it becomes history. Privacy concerns are widespread and troubling, with historical events making the general public willing to sacrifice privacy for safety. As Benjamin Franklin once said: "*Those who would give up essential Liberty, to purchase a little temporary Safety, deserve neither Liberty nor Safety.*"

The use of technology can also negatively impact attention spans and physical health or lead to mental health issues, such as lack of empathy, damaged self-esteem, anxiety, depression, and other problems. Society needs to catch up and better address the threats and opportunities. Consider how many jobs may disappear as we implement computers to perform those functions. Though many jobs may vanish, new positions will also emerge, as has always been the case throughout history.

I highly recommend using the abundance of information available for higher learning to stay as informed as possible about the advances in technology that we are all using and adapting to on a daily basis. Otherwise, you may quickly fall behind. This exponential growth in technology can either save us or destroy us, so it is crucial to find a balance. Don't get left behind, but also don't become consumed by it.

Build Your Library

Become a student of life! Learn about economics, history, law, accounting, spiritualism, culture, finance, travel, language, etc. Unlearn doubt and negativity. Minimize, organize, and maintain simplicity. Focus daily on the vision you wish to achieve and believe that it is on its way to you as long as you consistently steer it in the right direction.

You know what you want to happen, now maintain the simplicity of mind and dedication to the success of whatever you're striving to achieve. Develop unwavering faith in yourself and the idea that success, whatever it may be, will come. If you do this without doubt or negativity, anything is possible.

No matter what beliefs you hold—whether they are religious, non-religious, scientific, or otherwise—your ability to bring your vision to life depends on the level of faith and commitment you invest in it. Strength can be drawn from a higher power or found within yourself, but it's your belief that grants power to the vision you're focused on, allowing it to become reality. In much the same way that currency—whether euros, pesos, or dollars—holds value because we collectively believe in it, your intentional pursuit of life and your vision is built on your belief in its potential to become reality.

The Battle Within

It should come as no surprise that while rebuilding your foundation, you will face opposition from the old one. Nothing that lives wants to die, but sometimes death is necessary for creation. If you want freedom in your life, then it will be. The old foundation is an anchor tied to you, trapping you in a hole. You'll never get out of this hole unless you start climbing, and climbing out is impossible with that anchor tied to you, so it is necessary to let it go. The battle to let it go will only be won if you have faith that what you're trading it for is better than what you are leaving behind.

Life often presents forces that pull or push you away from your goals. Like a vortex, negative effects may try to draw you in and keep you stuck, while opposing forces may push you away from what you're striving for. You must stand your ground, determined to fight for what you know you want. Your ability to navigate these forces with determination will ultimately define your path and success.

What creates, heals, and energizes us is within a realm that relies on outside input to tell it what to do. Creation is based on our environment, and our environment is portrayed as we see it. Therefore, what we perceive and how we perceive it create an environment that is observed, interpreted, and delivered to everything which makes up our existence. Create a positive, healthy environment through your perception. Like fuel for a vehicle, you can tell the difference if the fuel is good or bad, so put in good fuel. If you have the information in this book stored in your mind, then when you do something out of character, you will question where it came from and why. You will also find yourself always nudging yourself back on the right track because you know it's necessary to do so.

If you've gotten to the point where you are comfortable leaving the past behind, building a new foundation, and have become confident and excited about the house you want to build, then you have set yourself on the path. It's your path, not someone else's, so take ownership of it. It only exists because of you and not only lives but thrives because of you as well. Take care of your vision of the path's direction as you would anything that you love. At this point, it's not about something that is afraid to die; it's about caring for it so that it doesn't.

Awareness

Awareness is liberation. In *The Zen Teaching of Bodhidharma: "Buddha is Sanskrit for what you call aware, miraculously aware."* To achieve true freedom, you must cultivate a level of awareness that instills confidence in yourself, your path, and your security, rather than succumbing to blindness and delusions.

Questioning your mind and following your desires for a life of peace and knowledge is necessary for personal freedom. When thoughts arise that don't fit into your personal narrative, you must have the mental strength to question them, break them down, and find out where they came from and why. Battling these thoughts may lead you to add or adjust steps on the path to your goals. Make small changes to your steps if necessary, but be cautious with changing goals, as they are like mile markers on your path. Changing them allows the monkey mind to influence your decisions and potentially your direction. Your goals are the anchors that keep you grounded, while the steps are the flexible actions that guide you toward them.

If you begin to change those goals, make sure you're not just opening one of the other doors out of fear, lack of education, or curiosity. There will be a reason you feel the need to take a different path from the one you determined, and it will usually have something to do with the "white noise." Question it and determine its truth. Are you being dissuaded? Are you acting out of fear? Can you overcome these obstacles and regain your confidence? By looking inward and filtering out external influences, you can reaffirm your chosen path.

Decisions in life are made easier by the understanding and confidence you have in what you want. This will create an assertiveness to see it come to fruition. If you decide to make a choice that changes that path, you have lost some of the faith you had in it. If you realize later that you were wrong, it can cost you a lot more time and energy to get back to it than if you had just maintained your course confidently.

Awareness quiets the mind and calms the spirit. It blocks out the noise and connects you to what is living, not created. If you find an expanded awareness of yourself and reality, then you won't be depressed for yourself, but sad for other objects in the world (other people, animals, the Earth itself). You don't find anxiety within yourself; you'll feel it from others because of that awareness and acceptance.

When you live the life you've chosen, put your house in order, strive to achieve the goals that you've set on your path, and do not fear death, you have peace of mind, accepting that you're doing the best you can with the hand you were dealt. But this is the construction of a foundation after a catalyst brings you understanding. That internal peace is hard to find. Reading scripture or philosophy may provide conceptual ideas, but the truth lies within you, elevated by your awareness of what surrounds you.

There is a path to this state of mind described in many ways using many different metaphors, but they don't make sense unless you're reading them in retrospect from what you understand to be the teaching. Just as I have found in writing this book, it is extremely difficult to describe this mentality in an understandable way; it must be felt to be understood.

I'd experienced loss before, but never had the freedom. I'd had moments of freedom, but without the weight of immediate loss or the search for something more. I'd been a seeker without true freedom, and I never really expected to face death, even when it was a reality. Like most people, I encountered these situations at different times, but it is the way they happen—and the timing of how they unfold—that opens the door.

The best one can do is to inspire others to seek answers from within, offer ideas to help them break free from a life that binds them in chains, and guide them toward freedom and truth on their journey to understanding, acceptance, and connection. I first wanted to express the ideas that guide you there, so you can reflect, study, and truly understand.

While discovering this "way of all things" that provides internal peace, I was initially unaware of the profound philosophical or religious ideas behind it. It was only after reading many books, spanning different cultures and generations, that I truly began to understand the deeper congruence of it all. This realization now compels me to describe and share it with the world to the best of my ability.

In reference to the quote in chapter two, don't be too quick to read the text and assume it won't work for you because of the intense pressure that your environment (or "box") imposes on you—it is *within* you. If you study with the hope of gaining awareness through reading, you're going backward. Reading the literature makes sense because you are aware; awareness doesn't primarily come from being literate.

On your journey, before you reach that place, before your dreams come true, and before you find that feeling, let me leave you with this: The day is yours! Every day is yours to shape into what you want it to be. A negative perception can create a negative experience, just as a positive perception can transform your day for the better. Tell yourself: *"I want my goals to become reality, and I will fight to make it happen. Through my positive perception, constant learning, openness, understanding, and my will to make it so, every passing day is an opportunity to move in the direction I desire—otherwise, I'm just wasting time."*

Chapter 10

"Characteristics of the rational soul: Self-perception, self-examination, and the power to make itself whatever it wants. It reaches its intended goal, no matter where the limits of its life is set."

- Marcus Aurelius

Challenge your mind and the source of its logic. Strive to become a better version of yourself for your own sake. Become excited about the person you aspire to be and eagerly seek the knowledge necessary to become that person. Have faith and understanding that it *is* possible, recognizing that belief in potential is a powerful catalyst for transformation. By doing so, you start to transcend conventional boundaries. If you can find your way to climb the mountain, take on its energy, and ask yourself profound questions for deeper understanding, you are fostering a connection with the essence of your being and beginning to peek outside of the box.

Outside of the Box

I can show you the map, plot the course, and tell you what you'll find, but I can't make you take the journey; it's up to you. There are many ways to climb the mountain, and you should find your own path, but the stories, concepts, and ideas described here will at least inform you of one way to get there. You can take that path, a different path, or find your own way. Either way, you'll have to take the first steps if you want to get there. To reach a place where your mind is free, delusions are absent, awareness peaks, and your path is clear.

Once you've reached your freedom of mind, you'll be living two different lives: one that is necessary for society, and one that follows your path to freedom. Looking outside the box and building the person you aspire to be in that reality marks the beginning of your journey toward a fulfilling and authentic life. The first significant step for myself was letting go of the need to control everything and instead start observing. The next step was to immerse myself in new environments, becoming a random person in a random place, surrounded by people who didn't know me. This taught me humility, showing me that my identity didn't matter as much as the character I embodied. The third was time. The fact that I didn't owe my time to anything or anyone gave me the freedom to let things be as they would be, no matter the outcome.

I've used several quotes in this book from people who've done just what I'm asking you to do for yourself, as I have discovered on my journey. Try to free your mind and understand who you are. Look around at the magnificence of the world around you. Understand what you can change and what you cannot. When you realize the freedom of your true self, then any question you ask will give you the same answer a Buddhist monk would meditate on, an American philosopher would discover, a Roman Stoic would come to find, or could be derived from the ideas of Christianity, Islam, Hinduism, etc.

I believe that if you can remove the silly distractions in life and boil everything down to its simplest most basic thoughts, you will come to the same understanding as anyone would, anywhere, throughout time. The principles are basic, and we are all equal in these simple principles. *"The softest thing in the universe overcomes the hardest thing in the universe. That without substance can enter where there is no room. Hence I know the value of non-action. Teaching without words and work without doing are understood by very few."- Lao Tzu*

These simple truths are not something that can be shown or told to someone. They must be experienced and felt to be understood. By reducing distractions and outside influences that dictate what you should do, who you should be, and what is acceptable, you can search within yourself for understanding. While we must live in the world that exists and do what is necessary to survive, our minds are capable of great things. It doesn't take a lot of brainpower or experience to understand the basic fabric of everything, but it can only be seen if you remove the substance that shadows your ability to see it. Otherwise, you could be left with an internal void, a feeling of emptiness as if something is missing, loneliness, a lack of purpose, or unfulfilled desires.

Faith and Purpose

Before becoming "Dictator Perpetuo," after nearly a decade away from Rome, Julius Caesar made an irreversible decision with significant consequences: to cross the Rubicon River with his army. Knowing that crossing this border of the Roman Empire into Italy proper represented "marching on Rome," a potential death sentence, he did so with determination.

This is about making decisions that align with your purpose, instead of being concerned about retreat. It is a dedication to achieving success. Let no one or nothing sway you from the vision of your future. Vision becomes destiny, and destiny becomes reality when you fully embrace the vision, set goals with unwavering faith, and refuse to let anyone derail your focus.

More people are moving away from faith, and as a result, it seems we are becoming more lost. Why is that? Why are we drifting further from faith and religion? Perhaps we are starting to question or sense that what we have been taught to believe doesn't feel right. I have spoken with many who believe that nothing happens after death and are leaning toward a more atheistic perspective on life and death, seeing things in black and white. As mentioned in "Aim for the Middle," the path of least resistance is where the lines blur, where it is most certainly gray.

An example of this concept is a friend of mine who took a democratic stance in a predominantly republican household, causing significant conflict and tension. I explained that being independent means listening, observing, educating yourself, and making decisions based on your true beliefs. This brought relief and a sense of reality to my friend, based on a deeper understanding of the situation. While they agreed with some of their parents' political views, they felt it was important to stand firm on the opposite side.

Just as with atheism, some people may feel that if they disagree with certain aspects of Christianity, Islam, or Judaism, they must reject them entirely and believe in nothing. Believing in nothing, or in nothing happening after death, can be a catalyst in itself. Those who have faith move forward with purpose. Faith or belief provides internal strength and guidance like a compass. If you don't believe in anything, believe in yourself, because faith in what will happen can give you purpose and drive, making anything achievable.

There is a wealth of information in the world about these concepts, but how they are presented may not always resonate with everyone. It depends on an individual's influences and perceptions of life. If you identify as Christian and not Buddhist, you may never explore the similarities between the two, just presented in different ways. The gray areas help the black and white coexist harmoniously. What are you afraid of? Confusion, fear, disloyalty? It may be easy for me to say, as I have always lived my life in the middle, seeking to understand and weigh variables against common sense and knowledge. But, if you strive to find your true self, you will discover the direction you need, and your faith in that path will be your compass.

Where & Why

Where does your journey begin, and why? If you feel hopeless, always consider that large processes take small steps to achieve. Whether it's a small amount of money, a small sacrifice in time, or some leisure activity, it will get easier. The most important thing is to start and remind yourself *why* you felt the need to start in the first place. "*Making a choice that is 1 percent better or 1 percent worse seems insignificant in the moment, but over the span of moments that make up a lifetime these choices determine the difference between who you are and who you could be. Success is the product of daily habits—not once-in-a-lifetime transformations.*" - *James Clear*

This difficult journey is about your freedom, peace of mind, protection, and the protection of those you love. Nothing is more important. Do what you will for the right reasons. Why are you doing it? What do you hope to achieve? When you act for something greater than yourself with purpose and principle, you won't fail to accomplish it. By offering something—a fair trade—with good intention, it will come to you because you know why you're doing it. When you succeed, you will have peace of mind because of that.

Where will the road lead you? Can you accomplish what you desire from where you are? Will you change it all to begin somewhere new with the prospect of a "leg up" in terms of time, money, or mental health? What is required to get you to that place, and how long will it take to acquire it? Patience. Remember that every setback or challenge is an opportunity to refine your approach and strengthen your resolve, and each small victory, however minor it may seem, is a step closer to achieving your larger goals.

Take the time to understand all of the angles. Do the necessary research and attempt to gain wisdom from others who have already experienced what you will. Where there is a will to succeed, there is a way. If your vision is strong enough, then you know why you are working toward that goal, and that has created your will to succeed and shown you the way. That is your purpose and direction.

The Point of No Return

Without loss, one does not gain the mindset. Being kicked off the wrong track can lead to discovering the right one. Reality is shaped by our experiences. If you don't realize you're on the wrong path and take steps to change, you may never find the right one. If you experience moments described in this book—a change in your outlook on the world, a perception of what can be, the fruition of goals, and the ability to "let go" so as to let life play out like a force that you are a part of but not in control of—you can't go back. Who would want to?

This feeling of freedom and clarity is profound, but it can be fleeting, easily overshadowed by the pressures of life and the influence of those around you who may not fully grasp what you're trying to express—because it defies simple explanation. Humans tend to believe that things need to be complex to hold meaning, so they overcomplicate them. Those distractions must be managed by you in order to feel truly free within society.

Knowing that this state of being exists can make life more challenging as you navigate a world designed to obscure it. However, despite the struggle, it is vital to pursue your freedom, independence, and enlightenment. There is so much to see and experience in this world that it's worth every effort. Achieving this state is like the final touch on a masterpiece—the culmination of everything, a sense of true completion. When you experience this, coupled with the knowledge and practice of living a simple, humble, and explorative life—executed in your own way and for the betterment of the system as a whole—you feel oneness, acceptance: Nirvana. Call it whatever you want when it comes, but you will have reached the point of no return. It can change your life forever, and you won't be able to describe it.

Keep Your Mind Clear

Like a raw piece of material being forged in fire, through the vision and understanding of what it will be, a process starts to take place and a form starts to take shape. Then we can start to see even better in our mind's eye what it can be. Continuing to forge, shape, and sharpen until what we desire has been created from the raw materials into the sharpened sword: vision, structure, desire, determination, intention, perseverance...freedom.

Take the information in this book and adopt it—really try to use it. You'll find that when a question arises in your mind, there is an answer to be found within its lessons. Fight or flight instincts, unconscious thoughts, self-doubt, and self-pity. You must remind yourself (your own mind) of your purpose and direction until it becomes a definiteness of purpose. Every step on your journey will be a battle, and every goal a war. You don't need to be battling yourself as well; if that happens, one can truly begin to feel lost. Throughout the many transitions of life, the information in this book provides answers to any questions you may have during times of loss or confusion. It's comforting to know that there is never a roadblock you can't get through because you have answers to the questions you face. It is my hope that others will find the information comforting, useful, mind-expanding, and deeply inspirational.

To have the freedom of mind, to simply tune out all of that noise by seeing it for what it truly is. To look at it is to make it go away. The situations that many of us find daunting, depressing, deplorable, and in some situations just plain evil, will go away if we as a whole take that power away by giving power to ourselves. Find your path, for yourself. Recognize the delusional world that is programming your thoughts and moves every day, and walk away. You can't see the stars in the sky when the city lights skew your vision. Or, as some might say, what if God is speaking to you, but you just can't hear over the noise?

"If you can cut free of impressions that cling to the mind, free of the future and the past-can make yourself, as Empedocles says, "a sphere rejoicing in its perfect stillness," and concentrate on living what can be lived (which means the present)... then you can spend the time you have left in tranquility. And in kindness. And at peace with the spirit within you." - Marcus Aurelius

CHAPTER 11

"The more sand has escaped from the hourglass of our life, the clearer we should see through it."
- Niccolo Machiavelli

In your life, if you are fortunate enough to play the game for a long period of time, you will experience the death of others, the feelings of love and loss, the experiences of youth, and the wisdom of old age. There are so many questions and concepts to ponder, educate yourself upon, and possibly contribute to.

As it stands for you now, you have everything in abundance and are surrounded by it. The simple concept of the apple in Eve's hand, the idea that we want what we can't have, is a reality that will come to you when it's too late. Most likely, when you die, you won't have the ability to see and feel what is so beautiful and plentiful now. Like supply and demand, when something is abundant, it will be taken for granted, and when it is in short supply, it becomes much more valuable.

Occupy

How will you occupy your time after you've reached the top of your mountain? You may have heard stories of people who worked their entire lives and then passed away shortly after retirement. I've had conversations with some who have found that there *is* a shock to the system when there is no daily driver to keep them moving. Imagine what can be accomplished in just one day, like the story I shared in Chapter 1. Now, think of a time in your life when an entire week passed by quickly due to boredom or, in some cases, depression.

Two statements have been made in this book regarding this concept. Firstly, we are all dealt the same amount of cards (time in a day). How time passes in your perception is relative to the amount of activity you accomplish. The second concept is related to time management and building your game plan. If you set out several tasks to do or a place to visit, you will achieve more on that day than someone who aimlessly wanders around trying to find something to do. At the end of a week, one person could proudly say they visited six states, four national parks, created an album of memories, and will feel more fulfilled than the other person whose week flew by with a vague recollection of individual days and minimal accomplishments.

Why did one day seem to pass faster than the other when both individuals were given the same amount of time? The answer lies in relativity. Einstein determined that time is relative—in other words, the rate at which time passes depends on your frame of reference and what is observed and experienced in one instance versus another. Philosophically speaking, if you want twenty years to feel like a flash after achieving your goals, aim to do nothing more than what you have already accomplished. Without new challenges or goals, time may seem to pass quickly and uneventfully, whereas actively pursuing new goals and experiences makes time feel richer and more meaningful

Forget about the image of sitting on a beach all day. The reality of that situation is that you'll become bored after one week and start looking for something to do. Imagine spending fifty years working toward the idea of sitting on that beach, only to find that you become bored within a week. The best way to utilize your time is to fill it with as much as you can achieve, preferably for the betterment of the future for all who may be involved.

"When Andrew Carnegie died, they discovered a sheet of paper upon which he had written one of the major goals of his life: to spend the first half of his life accumulating money and to spend the last half of his life giving it all away. And he did!" - Jim Rohn

Finding something to occupy your time can take various forms. Some find that by accumulating wealth, they can provide greater fortunes for future generations. Others dedicate their lives to helping others or supporting great causes. The influences, passions, and perceptions of life will guide the path each person takes. Find a sense of self in this life, something long-lasting that you are a part of, something you can contribute to. Build something that will exist beyond your time, something for which you will hopefully be remembered. Give yourself the freedom in this life to know that when you move on to the next round of this game, whatever it may be, you have at least played this round the best you could and are happy with what you have accomplished and for what you leave behind.

End Game

It has all gone according to plan, even better than you imagined. Hindsight is 20/20. If you can imagine standing where you hope to be and looking back, you would know that your visions turned into goals and your determination, focus, and perseverance were determining factors that brought you to this place. You've manifested your destiny, but how far into the future did you look? You will need some sort of motivator to become successful in your desires. Something that *pulls* you toward the life you imagine, through the inevitable hardships, losses, and obstructions. As success brings you wealth and power, consider a memento to keep yourself humble after achieving your desired goals. It's not about reverting; it's about appreciating. Hardships endured over time can mold a person into a powerful force of contempt and disregard, which, if untethered, can cause harm to itself.

"He who makes a beast of himself gets rid of the pain of being a man." - Samuel Johnson

Aiming for balance and maintaining awareness is about understanding not to forget where you came from or the journey that led you to where you are now. Remember that there are always others out there striving to achieve, feeling lost, or in pain. They fall down and pick themselves up, just as we all do on our journey to find purpose while we move toward an uncertain end.

A solitaire card game serves as my own memento. During a time when I was deeply immersed in a journey toward self-understanding, a friend let me use his "bridge." It was during a transitional period of my life, but I was open to everything and everyone. I met so many great people in his environment, and it made me happy—happy to have a friend that would offer me a place to be, and for every small thing in the world that was joyful. As I contemplated life and let these "outside of the box" ideas come to mind and flow onto paper, I played cards often, and those cards began to symbolize valuable lessons. Now, as a regular part of my morning routine, I go through that same motion every day and recall a time when my happiness stemmed from simply experiencing life, without needing validation from affection, possessions, or money. "I am," I said. I am happy in this vehicle (body), in this place, and with whatever happens, and that's enough.

Can you live a life that wouldn't be changed by money? Is the life that you intend to create for yourself going to change if someone offered you all the money you could stand or took it all away? If you have true freedom of mind and walk the path you determined, can you have the house on the hill while being just as content if you didn't have it? That's freedom. The acceptance and joy in life from being able to live in such a way that it doesn't depend on something to fulfill it. Like the card game, how would you know what to do if you don't get that card that you want? You still need to be able to enjoy the fact that it's just a game.

You *will* find a way to be free—free from influence, distraction, and demands from outside forces. Then, you will seek to understand yourself, who you are, and what makes you happy in the simplicity of natural things in life. Finally, you will embrace the peace of living in each moment, with the realization and acceptance of your destiny as well as your fate.

When you have given up everything and accepted it, understand the world around you and your place in it, with a true understanding of who you are, reach a calmness of mind in living for the moment, and accept that death may come at any one of those moments, then you will see. Anywhere you are, at any point in time, should be a good place to die on a beautiful day. When you wake in the morning, rested and at peace with yourself, with a place for everything and everything in its place, start the day grateful for all the possibilities—and for your ability to experience them. Greet the day with anticipation of finding ever-changing beauty and complexity in whatever it may bring. When you live the life you have chosen, put your house in order, and do not fear death, this is peace.

What Now?

How do I live my life now that's different from before the freedom catalyst? I observe and question everything. I constantly strive to understand not only the external world but also my internal motivations, using the principles described in this book as my guide. Focus is a discipline that grows stronger with practice, so it's not uncommon for me to question my thought processes. It's not uncommon for me to weigh the thoughts I'm having against the decisions that I've made, and it's not uncommon for me to stop, pause, and reset my focus so I can walk past doors that I'm curious about. Curiosity is powerful, but intentionality is what brings true progress.

I have introduced chaos and, in turn, created calm and clarity. I have thrown away the future and, in turn, see the path. I have accepted the end of my life, and it has become more beautiful and full of possibility. Peace isn't found in controlling every outcome, but in trusting the journey itself. If your well-being matters to you, be your own savior while you can—there is no one else more invested in your success. Anything done consistently, daily, becomes fulfilled faster than just the thought of its fruition.

Do what you can for yourself, because if you can do it and inspire someone else to do the same, both of you will contribute to the spread of individualized freedom. When we collectively inspire change through action, we can move forward faster than if we procrastinate, stuck in the belief that change will never come. When the "changed" outnumber the unchanged, then we will see *real* changes.

Self-deception is one of the greatest obstacles to freedom. You can't know your true mind if you deceive yourself, and as long as you deceive and are deceived, freedom is just an idea. You are not your job, your parents, a number, or a statistic. You *are* a miracle with an opportunity to explore the concepts of existence by knowing your deepest self, and in doing so, becoming aware of the true reality around you, as many others have before you. Then, you'll be the one to tell them that you can't explain it, but it exists within all of us.

Who are you? Are you different from before you read this? What will your reason be, and what is your compass? Do you *feel* life, or just exist within it? What is your nature? What is your dream? Ponder long and well the questions that need to be answered to see the reality that exists beyond the smokescreen.

Conclusion

What I say is something that many have said before in various ways. Perhaps this book will help you understand it, or maybe the tenth book with a similar concept will help you piece it together like a puzzle for your own comprehension. When I embarked on a journey with an open mind and many questions, repeatedly asking and reviewing answers, I gained confidence in my understanding, what I needed to do, and the direction I was headed. I have no doubt that you can reach the same conclusion.

Remember these four factors: **Loss, freedom, sense of self, and acceptance of fate.** I had traveled many times before and had seen many beautiful things, but had never had a feeling like this. The first time it came on like an engine that started to run and then sputtered out. A form of letting go, like the analogy of the river earlier in the book, or you could imagine surfing, when you're paddling against the wave and then pulled by it. It made me well up and start to laugh because so much "weight" had been lifted. The second time it came, the engine was running on all cylinders; you rise against the wave and as you instinctively take on its energy and move with it, you flow as one.

I have found that many civilizations at many points in history all came to similar conclusions when they asked themselves the questions that naturally arise from the mind that searches for true answers. It doesn't matter what point in history it was, what was happening in the world at the time, or how they decided to portray it. Through art, haikus, philosophy, or written words in text or music, it is a truth that is discovered from within, an understanding of complexity through simplicity.

Find yourself as part of the universe, experiencing a profound connection that is challenging to describe but overwhelming in its beauty, heightening your awareness. I hope we all reach this place, as it would be the change we've long awaited. As stated in Chapter 1, "It waits for you to open the door," and if you seek it, you will find it. To merely find it and return is survival, but to find it and remain, or strive to find it again, is to truly live.

The confidence I gained from discovering this truth sparked my interest in becoming a more knowledgeable person. From philosophy to romance, finance, history, and more, the concepts I encountered were interwoven through all types of information. Removing distractions and categorizations allows you to perceive the simplicity at the core of all things, connecting like the entire tree—its roots, leaves, ecosystem, and reasoning all stem from the seed.

"Rise, awake! Having obtained your boons, understand them! The sharp edge of a razor is difficult to pass over; thus the wise say the path (to the self) is hard."

- Katha Upanishad

I leave you with a personal journal entry of mine, something that was written after a moment of reflection, that startled me as if someone else had written it, becoming one of the inspirations for this book. It offers a glimpse into a mind seeking answers.

"The face hasn't changed much, but the eyes have. What we experience, learn, explore, and ponder from one life to the next enriches our soul, our spirit, and can be felt by any source of energy in varying degrees, depending on the consciousness level of the material object that embodies that energy. For two years, you have been searching for answers and asking questions; this is the beginning, the necessary first step to reaching an enlightened state of mind.

What are the questions?

Who am I? *You are the result of your peers, observations, tutelage, your feelings based on subconscious understanding, and the choices and decisions made from that understanding.*

Why am I here? *Without knowledge of where you are, how you got there, or which direction to go, it's hard to know where you're going without a compass—assuming you even know how to use the compass. That has been life up to this point.*

What is the compass? *Faith and meaning. While observing multiple philosophies and religions, I have found that Buddhism, Hinduism, Stoicism, Roman, and American philosophies all share common traits. There is a necessary balance. There is a state of mind to be achieved. There is order in chaos. It's a game to be played where the understanding from one place takes you to another for further learning.*

What do I want? *This question is difficult to answer when battling a subconscious mind that 'thinks' it knows what you're 'supposed' to be doing. You should do what makes you happy first and foremost. You will only enjoy doing something if it motivates you to become better at it—the desire for perfection through constant adaptation and learning.*

Where do I want to go? *I once felt that I must experience all the options before making a decision like this, but the answer is much simpler than I had originally thought. You should go where you are treated best, where you can be happy every day practicing your art, so you are not distracted in the pursuit of that perfection.*

To summarize: *the question 'Who am I?' is to be answered with 'Who do you want to be?' The question 'Why am I here?' is to be answered with 'To learn as much as possible, not for who you are now, but for who you will become.' The question 'What will I do?' is to be answered with 'You will do whatever you desire to be great at; learning comes from the perfect execution of what you aspire to achieve.' The question 'Where will I go?' is to be answered with 'Go where your heart desires, where you can pursue these goals happily, without interrupting their progress.' Find a hub that helps you achieve those goals. Nothing seems to dampen progress more than the monkey mind.*

Remember, this journey began with the freedom to ask these questions and make decisions freely. The desire for money is not a desire for money itself; it is a desire for freedom. In letting go of everything, I have experienced a level of freedom that is both enlightening and shocking to the mind and soul, leading me to the mental place I am in now. Project yourself to your death—that is where you'll find the meaning of your life. Be prepared for death always; in death, we find true meaning. In facing death, we experience the most life."

Thank you for taking this part of your journey with me. I hope that you now know *why* you must continue the journey from here on your own and that you understand the concepts regarding *awareness* of yourself, direction of *intent*, and the *compass* that will guide your boat to your individualized *freedom* of mind and body.

Living every moment intentionally makes your decisions easier, removes the weight of uncertainty from your shoulders, and allows you to flow through every moment like a wave, with massive energy, yet in simplicity.

If you have found this book to be helpful to you and believe it may be beneficial to others, kindly leave a review if you can. This will encourage others to start their journey as well.

Remember, if you can do it and inspire someone else to do it, both you and they will continue to contribute to individualized freedom. By sharing that energy, we can reach our goals faster than if we procrastinate, thinking we will never change. When the "changed" outnumber the unchanged, that's when we will see *real* changes.

INDEX

A

acceptance, 12, 36, 89–90, 93, 115, 127–128, 139, 146, 149
adversity, 37, 105
anger, 7, 14, 16, 69, 89, 103
anxiety, 27, 45, 50, 53–54, 62, 69, 87, 90, 108, 123, 127
Aurelius, Marcus, 90, 131, 140
auto-pilot decision, 56
awareness, 7, 11, 17, 87–88, 113, 120, 126–129, 132, 145, 150, 155

B

bad luck, 57–58
basic principles, 52, 98–100, 105
behavioral patterns, 104
blood-thirsty patrons, 14
Buddha, 47, 61, 126
Buddhist, 109, 133, 136
business model, 114

C

Caesar, Julius, 134
catalyst, 10–11, 13, 25, 65, 118, 120, 128, 131, 135, 147
changing goals, 126
Christianity, 109, 133, 135
complexity, 147, 150
confidence, 4, 39–40, 42, 126–127, 149–150
Confucius, 71, 96
conscious decision, 24
consciousness, making sense of, 26
constants, 52, 55
crossroads, 63–65, 93
curiosity, 60, 98, 127, 147

D

deepest self, 148
depression, 45, 89, 102–103, 123, 142

desire, 41, 65, 67–68, 72–74, 77, 86, 93, 134, 144, 152–153
determination, 33, 78, 84, 125, 134, 139, 144
different metaphors, 128
disease, 17, 27
Dyer, Wayne, 45

E

exercise, 24, 53, 79, 81–83, 91, 100
expectations of others, 39, 42, 116
exponential growth, 81, 121–123

F

failure, 27, 39, 55–56, 86
faith, 134–136
fear, 2, 9, 11–12, 72–73, 85–87, 90, 93, 104–108, 111, 127, 136, 147
fear of, 85–87
  dying, 86
  exposure, 86
  failure, 86
  uncertainty, 86
  unknown, 86
free-minded individual, 59
free time, 119
frustration, 14, 69, 87

G

game plan, 38, 44, 142
Gandhi, Mahatma, 97
grief, 89
  acceptance, 89–90
  anger, 89
  bargaining, 89
  denial, 89
  depression, 89

H

habitual systems, 24
happiness, 13, 31–32, 42, 52, 68, 75, 90, 92, 120, 145
health, 43, 83, 90, 122, 137
Heraclitus, 109
human beings, 95, 119
humility, 11, 25, 66, 86, 93, 98, 105, 110, 132

I

ideas, outside of the box, 27, 118, 131–133, 145
important factors:
  acceptance of fate, 149
  freedom, 149
  loss, 149
  sense of self, 149
individual freedom, 28, 98
inspiration grabs, 27
intelligence, 105, 121
intention, 74–75

internal peace, 128–129
Islam, 133, 135
isolation, 103

J
joy, 38, 78, 92, 146
Judaism, 109, 135

K
Kierkegaard, Soren, 88
knowledge, 73–78
Kubler-Ross, Elisabeth, 89
Kung Fu, meaning of, 99–100

L
life:
   delusions, 110, 126, 132
   lessons, 62
love, 14, 73–74, 89–91, 119–120, 126, 137, 141

M
Machiavelli, Niccolo, 141
manifestation, 98
middle way, 109–111
monkey mind, 106–107, 126, 153
morning routine, 83, 91, 145
motivating yourself, 25, 96
Musashi, Miyamoto, 19

N
necessary changes, 78
negative events, 73
Niebuhr, Reinhold, 49

O
obstacles, 35, 37, 51, 68–69, 127, 148
odds, 51, 57, 106

P
patience, 14, 27–28, 35, 71–72, 96, 98–101, 104, 121, 137
peace, 1, 4–5, 37, 67–68, 74, 79–80, 126–129, 137, 140, 146–147
perceptions, 11, 45, 69, 136, 144
personal:
   development, 4
   growth, 23, 31–32, 35, 48
   narrative, 126
Peterson, Jordan, 102
phases of mind:
   conscious mind, 20–21
   subconscious mind, 20–21
   unconscious mind, 21
plan B, 80
Plato, 113

positive healthy environment, 125
pre-set condition, 94
procrastination, 76
purpose, 134–135

R
real changes, 148, 155
reality, 4, 10, 13–15, 102, 124, 127–129, 132, 134–135, 143, 148
relationships, 37, 46, 66, 87, 98, 111
resistance, 52, 105, 135
respect, 58, 92, 111
Rohn, Jim, 35, 143
routine, 5, 21, 24, 53, 76, 82–84, 91, 99, 145

S
scantiest fare, 110
scared money, 77
self:
  aware consciousness, 26, 30, 86
  awareness, 26, 59, 65, 74, 120
  check daily, 94
  discovery, 39, 48
  doubt, 139
  pity, 58, 103, 139
simplicity, 93, 110, 123, 146, 150, 155

skin in the game, 104–106
small changes, 104, 126
structure, 4, 11, 21–22
subscriptions, 79

T
technology, 121–123
time:
  consuming, 83
  management, 117, 142
  relativity of, 143
trust-based system, 8
Twain, Mark, 85
Tzu, Lao, 133

U
unconscious thoughts, 139
untrust, 69

V
vision, 5, 27–28, 77–78, 126, 134, 137, 139–140, 144

W
wealth, 90–92
white noise, 29, 53, 69, 76, 88, 103, 127
wisdom, 33–34, 48–49, 96, 109, 137, 141
workout, 83

Made in the USA
Monee, IL
08 November 2024

69641749R00095